Preaching in the
Small Membership Church

Preaching
in the Small
Membership
Church

LEWIS A. PARKS

Abingdon Press
Nashville

PREACHING IN THE SMALL MEMBERSHIP CHURCH

Copyright © 2009 by Abingdon Press

All rights reserved.

This book is printed on acid-free paper.

Library of Congress Cataloging-in-Publication Data

Parks, Lewis A.
    Preaching in the small membership church / Lewis A. Parks.
        p.   cm.
    ISBN 978-0-687-64584-8 (binding: paperback, adhesive, perfect : alk. paper)
    1. Preaching.   2. Small churches.   I. Title.

BV4221.P27 2009
251—dc22

                                                                        2008051606

All scripture quotations unless noted otherwise are taken from New Revised Standard Version of the Bible, copyright 1989, Division of Christian Education of the National Council of the Churches of Christ in the United States of America. Used by permission. All rights reserved.

Scripture noted as NIV taken from the Holy Bible, NEW INTERNATIONAL VERSION®. Copyright © 1973, 1978, 1984 by International Bible Society. All rights reserved throughout the world. Used by permission of International Bible Society.

09 10 11 12 13 14 15 16 17 18—10 9 8 7 6 5 4 3 2

MANUFACTURED IN THE UNITED STATES OF AMERICA

To my mother,
Mary Kathryn Parks,
who prefers small membership churches.
They ask more of her.

Contents

Acknowledgments

I am deeply grateful to the small membership churches of Pennsylvania and Maryland where I have served as a student pastor and as a full-time pastor. I confess that most of time I served them I was too young or otherwise ignorant to appreciate their particular constellation of the people of God. I am grateful to the preaching and worship faculty of Wesley Theological Seminary, Laurence Hull Stookey, William R. (Bobby) McClain, and Lucy Lind Hogan, who teach and model effective preaching in all sizes of churches and were kind enough to provide feedback as I wrote this book. Rebecca Scheirer of Wesley provided a second set of critical eyes for the manuscript in its various stages and helped make it more reader friendly. Finally, I am grateful to the many pastors of small membership churches whom I have known through the years. Their perpetual word of advice to me has proved invaluable: "keep it real."

Introduction

Worship is the most important thing small membership churches do. Preaching is the heart of that worship. At the front of the sanctuary is a pulpit, a lectern, or their predecessor, the preaching desk. This is the place where ordained ministers, licensed pastors, or lay speakers employed for a season roll up their sleeves, clean off their glasses, and work up a sweat trying to connect the Word of God and the people of God, often with the audacity of a surgeon trying to connect a severed vein or a lineman repairing a downed power line.

Drama builds into the moment. The congregation finishes its hymn, sits down, and scrunches around for a comfortable position. Bulletins are tucked in hymnals; children are given crayons and paper. The pianist or organist leaves the bench; the drummer silences the percussion. All eyes focus forward to a person who stands to speak. No matter what this person does in the next few minutes to fulfill or belie her or his high calling, most present have a sense that something extraordinary should happen. The person up front is supposed to become a vehicle through which Almighty God breaks into the noise of everyday life and speaks to the disciples of Jesus. The congregation is not assembled to hear that person up front recite a string of trite stories or impress with theological shoptalk, or ramble on about himself or herself. The congregation, as a whole and as individual members, waits for a word from the Lord.

Some today have written off the small membership church so totally that they cannot see the weekly drama of the preaching event that occurs there. A church has only one valid script, they say. It must get bigger. They insist there is only one measure for good preaching. It must lead to more services and bigger sanctuaries. This is an unfair appraisal. We must approach preaching in the small membership church more like anthropologists expecting cultural treasure than as conquistadors disappointed that the natives don't behave more like us. Week after week in roughly 75 percent of the churches in this country, in churches with fewer than one hundred in worship, a preaching event occurs and *something* happens. We must name that something and do what we can to move it toward excellence.

This is not to say that preaching in the small membership church does not have its unique challenges. Three in particular stand out. First, there is the preacher's limited time for sermon preparation. Perhaps the preacher is serving three or more churches at the same time with little or no staff support. Or perhaps the preacher, like Paul the tent maker, is employed full time in work outside the church and steals time to prepare the message early or late in the day.

Second, there are the less-than-studio-like conditions for speaking in many small membership church buildings: poor or no sound systems, bad acoustics, inadequate lighting, no provision for child care, and no capacity to project images that amplify the message. And these conditions prevail at a time when persons sitting straight-backed in uncushioned pews that creak have grown accustomed to viewing the polished productions of television and movies from plush theatre seats and home recliners with cup holders.

Third, there is the suspicion of the preacher as an outsider. Most small membership churches began and grew to adolescence without benefit of a resident clergy. Through the years they were served by short-term pastors, part-time pastors, and student pastors. In my denomination it is not that unusual for a small membership church that is 150 years old to list a heritage of fifty-plus pastors. Self-reliance has been a necessary virtue. Guarding against attachment was and is a tool for emotional survival. The smiling preacher educated in a faraway school may plan to turn us into something we are not, and in any case will not be here long.

But along with those unique challenges, the small membership church offers the preacher unique opportunities. The preacher will know the ongoing stories of most persons in the pews and will know how the message is likely to intersect those stories. What will the parents who lost their five-year-old daughter to cancer hear when you preach about Jesus' healing of Jairus's little daughter from Mark 5? What will the couple who just lost the family farm hear when you talk about the rewards of good stewardship? Of course, such persons sit in congregations of all sizes, but their presence is accentuated in a small membership church. This has a way of keeping the sensitive preacher's language real.

The setting for preaching in a small membership church is charged in another, more subtle way. The question of the small membership church's place in the contemporary world is never far from the surface. Many congregations feel a collective shame that they have not grown appreciatively through the years. Some of these are waiting for someone from denominational headquarters to swoop down and close them as if they were a branch store that has operated in the red for too many years. Serious questions are worth asking in small membership churches, questions that reach to the nature and purpose of the church. Every sermon, whether pastoral or prophetic, apologetic or evangelical, has the potential to weigh in on the side of the worth of discipleship in a small membership church. The preacher who is savvy about this situation will have a special power in preaching.

Most small membership churches continue to hold the preaching act in high esteem. In many parts of the country, a congregation's favorite name for one who ministers among them is *Preacher*. I appreciate rather than try to correct this form of recognition when I hear it and will honor it in this book by viewing all other aspects of the pastoral office through the practice of preaching. As one who has a high view of the ordained office of ministry, I am well aware that you could make a similar case for focusing on the pastor as *Pastor*, as *Liturgist*, as *Leader*, or as some more generic term that holds them all together. But ordination is always also ordination to the Word, and it is pretty clear to me that connecting the people of God with the Word of God has to be at the center of any renewal of ministry in small membership churches today.

For more than five hundred years the churches with roots in the Reformation have insisted that one of the marks of the true church is that the Word is truly preached and heard. This book will explore ways to live out that mark in small membership churches.

We will start with the preacher as a student (chapter 1) sent by the congregation to search the Scriptures while sequestered in a study, using the best tools available, and practicing certain spiritual and intellectual disciplines. The preacher as anthropologist (chapter 2) diligently studies the congregation's stories, rituals, and artifacts in an effort to discern its corporate identity, its soul. The preacher as writer (chapter 3) combines the study of the Scriptures and the study of the congregation to create a manuscript that can be more or less memorized.

The preacher as speaker (chapter 4) maintains a teachable spirit in the art of connecting with the congregation through body, voice, and face. While immersed in the Bible's meta-stories, the preacher as storyteller (chapter 5) helps the congregation remember its story of corporate providence, a critical first step for transformation in many small membership churches today. The preacher as theologian (chapter 6) approaches experience as a reflective practitioner, acts as a guide for the corporate journey of faith, and provides the small membership church with a theological language for talking back to its critics. The preacher as leader (chapter 7) helps the small membership church summon its collective inner resources in order to face rather than deny its most difficult challenges.

The preacher as pastor (chapter 8) equips the congregation for the ministry of all Christians where gifts of healing abound while uniquely providing pastoral care for the body of Christ as a whole. The preacher as prophet (chapter 9) forth-tells and *fore*-tells in the small membership church where the saints and the sinners, the haves and the have-nots, the powerful and the marginal are packed together in incredibly tight quarters. And the preacher as evangelist (chapter 10) exchanges a worn-out model for disciple making for one that makes the most of a healthy small membership church's fundamental strengths.

My overriding purpose in this book is to name practical concerns and offer specific advice for those who preach in small membership churches. I will engage certain themes of contemporary theology, homiletics, and mission *without* engaging their respective literatures, but I hope to do this in a way that entices the reader to explore further. A short list of next-step reading suggestions by chapter is at the back of the book.

The Preacher as Student of Scripture

I teach in a summer school for persons who were called into ministry in mid-life or later and do not have the resources, or health, or time to endure the rigors of the ninety-hour Master of Divinity program required for ordination in my denomination. Although there are exceptions (doctors, lawyers, teachers), most of these adult students have only a high school education or the GED equivalent. They answered the call while they were driving a truck, serving as a teacher's aide, selling insurance, managing a daycare facility, or managing the power tools section of a home improvement store.

They were disciples of Jesus before they answered the call to ministry, and they served as speakers and teachers in their home congregations. They studied the Bible to prepare for their service, but where and how? I love to listen to their stories. They would get up before dawn and study the Bible for an hour or two before they began the day's work. They would steal away over the lunch hour to work on Sunday's lesson. They would play CDs of James Earl Jones reading the Gospels while they drove their rig across Interstate 70 from Pennsylvania to Colorado.

And now these servants of God's Word find themselves in the most exhilarating role reversal imaginable: they are being paid to study the Bible! They are expected to sequester themselves on a regular basis so they might indulge in a search of the Scriptures. The amateur gets to turn pro! And nobody in the small membership church, neither the one who shares the preacher's blue collar hunger to grow by learning nor the professional who appreciates the privileges accrued by higher education begrudge them this basic act of seclusion behind every sermon.

Of course, some licensed pastors, like some of their ordained counterparts, are not up to the compliment. They will flit from one Urgent Task to another like a hummingbird seeking the next red blossom. They will run on empty, squeezing as many sermons as they can out of the lingering fumes of an earlier period of study. But for those preachers who are up to the call to study that sustains the call to preach, there is the weekly experience that Scripture is an effervescent source of stories, themes, images, and plots just waiting to be discovered and carried back to the community of faith.

There are several points where preaching has a heroic quality about it, and this is one of them. The preacher is aware of being signaled out by the community of faith for a dangerous mission to a distant place, like the dove Noah sends out to find dry land after the flood waters subside. Will you find any sign of hope for them this week? Will you be able to bring back to God's people some message from their Lord?

There is no guarantee that you will. Most experienced preachers will remember a miserable occasion or two of showing up empty-handed on Sunday morning after a week's worth of honest labor. You can try to cover—add hymns, meander through announcements, prolong that baptism—or you can confess it: "the Lord gave me the silent treatment this week" and allow the congregation a peek inside the peculiar prayer risks of your call. Either way the memories of such failures are saturated with shame, and the preacher will seek whatever help there may be to avoid repeats. There are tools and disciplines that increase the odds of success.

Tools

Before naming the tools of the trade, a word about the place where the preacher will use them, *the study*. If I am sent out weekly to search for a word from God for the people of God, I must have an environment that encourages concentration. In the floor plans of older parsonages and manses, a space was always made for the pastor's study, often smaller than a modern walk-in closet, but always there. Old pictures show a room stacked with books and magazines, cluttered with spectacles, pens, assorted knickknacks, and dominated by a ratty but comfortable chair for reading and a plain table or desk for writing. The light that fills a study is wistfully amber.

The study has been replaced by an office in many parsonages. An office is a room with a different heritage and a different mission. It is a place of commerce, a place for the exchange of information and goods. An office needs to be equipped with the things that will support that exchange, with phones, personal computers, and fax machines. Its furniture should promote attention and conversation: uniform, comfortable but not too comfortable, arranged in calculated angles. The light that fills an office is analytically white.

To adapt one of Winston Churchill's shrewd observations: we shape the rooms we occupy and then our rooms shape us. Preachers need offices because preachers are also administrators, counselors, and coworkers, but preachers never stop being preachers who need the type of space that will promote and absorb the very personal struggle of sermon seeking and sermon writing. A study is a space where Jacob can wrestle with the angel, vowing, "I will not let you go, unless you bless me" (Genesis 32:26).

The first tool the preacher as student of Scripture must take up in this study is a *church translation of the Bible* from its original languages of Hebrew (Old Testament) and Greek (New Testament). There are half a dozen or so of them available, but two have emerged as preeminent:

- New Revised Standard Version of the Bible, copyright 1989, by the Division of Christian Education of the National Council of Churches of Christ in the United States of America (NRSV)
- *Holy Bible: Today's New International Version*, copyright 2005 by the International Bible Society (TNIV)

A church translation is to be distinguished from a paraphrase. In a paraphrase, a person or group like a Bible society offers a version of the text with more attention to clear contemporary expression than to the meaning or intent of the original Hebrew and Greek language of the Bible. A number of paraphrases are in print, such as J. B. Phillips's *The New Testament in Modern English* (1958); Kenneth N. Taylor's *Living Bible, Paraphrased* (1971); the American Bible Society's *Good News: The Bible in Today's English Version* (1976); and more recently, Eugene H. Peterson's *Message: The Bible in Contemporary Language* (2002). Paraphrases are compelling. The flow of the text seems less inhibited. There is little theological shoptalk to get in the way. The contemporary jargon reaches up from the page like an old friend inviting you into the conversation. For all these reasons paraphrases are helpful when it comes to introducing a seeker to the Bible or for personal devotions or for unfolding a text in the sermon. But paraphrases are not the church's translation of the Bible and should not be used as if they were, as most writers of paraphrases are quick to point out. Paraphrases are not the primary version of the text the preacher studies in sermon preparation or reads in worship or preaches from in the pulpit.

That version will be the product of one of the church's major collective efforts as was the NRSV and the NIV, or the King James Version (KJV), their prototype written four hundred years ago. The NRSV and NIV represent the voice of a broad consensus of the church. The number of scholars engaged in the writing is large enough to ensure a faithful knowledge of all the relevant ancient Hebrew and Greek manuscripts. Those same scholars working collaboratively hammer out a careful rendering of that text into English. Persons representing all three of the church's forms of governance (episcopal, presbyterian, and congregational) have their say. So do those from across the entire theological spectrum. Partisan readings are smoothed down; eccentric interpretations fall by the wayside.

Those who create the major church translations of the Bible desire to connect with contemporary readers but hold that aim in greater tension with the aim of faithfulness to the Hebrew and Greek text. That means bumps remain in the text to be worked out by the preacher as student: vengeful prayers to be explained, seeming contradictions to be untangled, runaway sentences to be corralled into sensible punctuation. Seasoned preachers know that some of their best preaching begins as a run-in with a stubborn text.

One note on local church hospitality and translations: in recent years church translations of the Bible have helped introduce more gender inclusive language into the culture of the local congregation. The irony in some small membership churches is that the majority of members and leaders are women yet the nouns and pronouns the preacher uses when referencing persons in worship are exclusively masculine. Hearing the Psalmist declare how good it is when "kindred" rather than only "brothers" dwell together in unity (133:1) or hearing Paul appeal to both "brothers and sisters" (1 Corinthians 1:10) is a significant step toward honoring the equality of men and women under God.

The second tool the preacher as student of Scripture must take up is a collection of good contemporary commentaries. But what is "good"? Here are three questions that help. First, does this commentary represent the broader voice of the church or only one individual? The preacher who prefers the church translation to the paraphrase will prefer also a commentary that represents the church in its rich unity-in-diversity, or "one-ness." Flourishing in that unity-in-diversity is one of the traditional marks of the true church.

Second, is this commentary preacher friendly? The writers of some commentaries are like the narcissistic friend who invites you into a conversation that turns out to be their monologue. The scholar's love for the minutia of archeology, the nuances of word study, or the intricacies of some variant reading of the text could be contagious. And the preacher as student and teacher comes to know the love of learning for learning's sake when it comes to the Bible. But Sunday is coming so the preacher needs commentaries where application to the life of the disciple and the church are woven into the entire fabric of the commentary and not given as a brisk endnote or afterthought.

Third, does this commentary represent important contemporary trends in biblical scholarship? There is a place for knowing how the church of the past read the Bible. What questions did they bring to the text? How did they try to be responsible to their time and place when they approached the Scripture? But each generation of biblical scholars builds on the work of their teachers, and it is important for the preacher to be in dedicated conversation with the biblical scholars of the present generation.

It might be tempting for the preacher who has received little or no formal theological training to settle for a paperback reprint of a popular commentary from the nineteenth century. Or perhaps it is the handsome multivolume hardback set of commentaries from the middle of the twentieth century, the gift from a retired pastor. What that preacher would miss for lack of acquaintance with more recent biblical scholarship is substantial. The preacher would miss the energy for preaching released by more recent schools of biblical study that find a way to move past the analytical knots created by earlier ways of thinking. She or he would miss the imagination for preaching released by those who invite us to inhabit the parables of Jesus rather than simply decode them as an earlier generation was determined to do. She or he would miss the passion for preaching released when a church experiencing decline begins once more to read the call to discipleship in its sacred texts.

I call the third tool for the study of scripture *a collection of voices from below.* One of the smartest things a leader of a congregation or any organization can do is to listen for the occasional telling remarks that come from persons who are often overlooked at the table of power where decisions are made. There is the new member who carries an outsider's perspective, the former addict who has no time for social politeness when it masks codependent behavior, or the teenager whose view of the world is so at odds with that of the generation who is running things.

These voices from below dampen our self-congratulatory moments of victory. Just about the time we think we have covered all the bases and tied up all the loose ends, one of these voices says something that jars us into silence, then sends us back to work. So why should we listen to them? There are two good reasons. First, "the church is ever reforming" (*ecclesia semper reformanda est*). This powerful little phrase was a gift to the church of all ages from the church leaders of the sixteenth century. Until the Kingdom comes and God's will is done on earth as it is in heaven the church's forms and structures are at best provisional. They are subject to scrutiny and open to revision. Listening to the voices from below is one of the best ways for the church to remain open to its environment, receiving life-saving cues to change and adapt.

Second, the voices from below represent the future of the church in its unity-in-diversity. The church that is shrinking toward a monoculture of age, gender, class, race, or ethnicity is a church flirting with death. A church moving toward a multicultural community of faith, however labored the steps (Acts 10), is a church running to catch up with the Spirit out ahead. The voices from below may not represent where most of us in the church are coming from today, but they do represent significant constituencies that must be present if the church is to flourish tomorrow.

As a leader must learn to listen to the voices from below, so must the preacher as student of the Scripture. The inner conversation might sound something like this: I will own and cherish the books that are the staples of my weekly sermon preparation, the translations and paraphrases, the commentaries, study Bibles, and books of illustrations. But I will also maintain a shelf of books that upset me too much ever to become a steady diet. For conscience's sake, I will make myself pick up one of them regularly and allow its voice to disturb my settled ways of reading the Bible.

In the setting of the middle class, mainline church where many of us begin, those voices might include (1) an African American reading of the Bible that stirs up ancient wounds, (2) a woman-centered reading of the Bible that questions contemporary power arrangements, (3) a reading of the Bible where the divine mandate that there "should be no poor among you" (Deuteronomy 15:4 NIV) is shown to be the Rosetta Stone for a multitude of texts, (4) a reading of the Bible by churches in nations subject to past and present oppression from other nations, or (5) an emerging-church reading of the Bible that is relentless in its criticism of the contemporary institutional church.

Disciplines

Some will argue that the preacher needs to maintain a personal devotional life of studying Scripture separate from the weekly discipline of seeking a word from God for the people of God. They worry that a person whose encounter with Scripture is driven by the need to produce for others will lose respect for the personal encounter with Scripture and compromise their sense of worth apart from work life. The preacher in the small membership church who is already pressed for time to read and write for preaching is given yet another reason to feel guilty for things left undone. If that preacher is bivocational, the sense that they have somehow lost their soul to the work of preaching may become so acute that they give up the call.

I want to offer some experience to the contrary, mine and that of a surprising number of preachers, once you get them to come clean about their solution to this conundrum. When I study for preaching, I am driven by the desire to find a word from God for the people of God. It is hard for me to imagine a more intense field of energy than that search. I tap into the depth of my call as one sent by the people to find a message. I tap into the mysterious chemistry by which faith is born in hearing the word preached. And I tap into the intercessory passion of carrying a people in my heart before God, the source of all our needs. Could there be a climate more favorable to personal prayers of thanks, confession, request, intercession, and praise than that?

When I write for preaching, I write with God looking over my shoulder as did Augustine writing in his *Confessions*. What starts as a search for right words soon becomes the search for true words, words that will stand before the One who knows my every flaw but calls me to this task just the same. The ultimate serious-ness of what I am doing is never far from the search for the mes-sage and the elements to support it. "Let the words of my mouth and the meditation of my heart be acceptable to you, O LORD, my rock and my redeemer" (Psalm 19:14).

I argue that the first discipline for preaching in the small mem-bership church is *to weave one's spiritual life into the reading and writing time of sermon preparation*. There are risks. The preacher is vulnerable to spiritual letdowns during the weeks away from preaching. They are not the pains of withdrawal from the kudos of a live audience for which they are sometimes mistaken, but a loss of spiritual intensity. Sermon preparation is a hothouse of spiritual growth. The preacher drops the seeds of her or his per-sonal stuff into the soil of public theological language and a crop springs forth to nourish both the preacher and the people of God on their spiritual journeys.

A second discipline the preacher as student of Scripture in a small membership church needs is *a commitment to preach from the full canon of Scripture*. It is a discipline to feed God's people from the full menu of the Bible's major food groups: the ancient stories of our forebears in the faith, the covenants between God and humans, the great books of Wisdom, the Prophets, the four Gospels, and the letters to the first Christian churches.

In the past some have insisted that the only way to do this faithfully is to use a formal list of texts for all the Sundays and special days of the church year (a lectionary). Others argued that they could be just as responsible to the full canon of Scripture while starting from some contemporary need or challenge to the faith provided they engaged in conscientious long-range plan-ning of their sermons. More recently many preachers have gravitated toward some combination of these two positions. They rely on a lectionary as the norm or fallback discipline while they experiment with thematic preaching. Or they find themselves on occasion turning from their normal practice of thematic preaching to the lectionary because they intuit some nearsightedness in their sermons.

There appear to be four common elements in this consensus, and the preacher as student of Scripture will want to pay attention to all four. First, the best way to commit to the full canon of Scripture is to have a long-range calendar for the texts of preaching. That calendar might be a traditional lectionary. Or it might be a contemporary thematic lectionary written by persons committed to the value of preaching "the whole purpose of God" (Acts 20:27). The preacher determined to come up with a homemade version of a preaching calendar must practice that commitment.

Second, a growing conviction on the part of many in the mainline church is that we can do better than we have been at reaching those beyond the walls of the church. To that end the old adage of communication still rings true: it's not so much what we say but what they hear that counts. The commitment to meet people where they are means that if and when we use the traditional lectionary we must move quickly from any in-house shoptalk ("when I first laid eyes on this week's lessons...") to language that grabs the seeker in the pews.

Third, at the same time there is a growing appreciation by many in the mainline church, and in other branches of the church, that the church's calendar of sacred seasons—Advent, Christmas, Epiphany, Lent, Easter, Pentecost—and the biblical texts that provide their form and content is a powerful tool for sustaining the community of faith as a counterculture. Disciples of Jesus learn to tell time in terms of the cycle of stories about Jesus and not just by the solar calendar.

A final discipline for the preacher as a student of Scripture is a *temperate use of the Internet.* In Christian tradition temperance is one of the four cardinal virtues, in addition to prudence, justice, and courage, found in Scripture and the wisdom teachings of many other ancient cultures. Temperance is the ability to regulate desires in the service of a higher purpose. It is moderation or self-control for the sake of a higher good. In the Bible, temperance is both a matter of exercising will power (Titus 2:12) and of receiving help from the Spirit who wants to see us manifest the fruit of a victorious life (Galatians 5:23).

When you sit down at a king's banquet, you *could* eat everything set before you, says the writer of Proverbs, but you'll regret the gorging afterward. Therefore, "put a knife to your throat" (Proverbs 23:2). At what point does the preacher using the Internet put that knife to his or her throat? Well, not too soon. Many of the tools the preacher needs are available online: dictionaries; encyclopedias; lectionaries and lectionary aids; search engines for quotes, illustrations, or images; plus, of course, an outline or the full-text sermon of gifted preachers from the next town over or a faraway continent. The Internet has drastically reduced the time and physical movement needed for this kind of preliminary research. There is no need for the preacher to scorn this gift.

But there are two points in sermon preparation when the preacher must back away from the Internet, must say no to the endless appetite for surfing in order to say yes to a higher purpose. First is for the sake of using good contemporary resources that are only available as books or CDs. The translations of the Bible, commentaries, and biblical studies identified above as necessary tools fall under this category because of the values they sustain. And the second reason is for the sake of claiming the integrity of one's own voice. We will unpack the work of finding an authentic preaching voice later, but a flag needs to go up here. There comes a time in every sermon preparation when what counts is not what somebody else hears God say through the text, however brilliant, colorful, haunting, or witty their words. What counts is what *this* particular preacher called to address *this* particular community of faith on *this* unrepeatable occasion hears God say.

2

The Preacher as Anthropologist

I was preaching on a three-point circuit of churches while the pastor recuperated from surgery. The third and final worship service of the morning was at the little Pfoutz Valley Church. I would rush out the door of the Millerstown church, jump into my car and hurry east on Route 17 along Wildcat Ridge, make a sharp turn left at Seven Stars Road, go about a quarter of a mile and turn right onto Township Road 549. Then I would ascend three hundred yards of narrow slate road leading to the small brick building set on a knoll overlooking dairy farms and state game land.

Pfoutz Valley turned two hundred in May 2007. It was started by a small group of farmers and a hearty circuit rider named Peter Beaver. It has worn at least five different denominational labels. Early in its history it transitioned from speaking German to English to attract new and younger members. It has prayed for and sometimes mourned its young men who fought in the Civil War, the two World Wars, the Korean War, the Vietnam War, the Gulf War, and now the Iraq War. The faint markings of separate men's and women's entrances can be spotted on the front of the building where inside today there is a healthy gender equality of leadership. The congregation has survived the loss of one building by fire, the turnover of forty-plus resident and nonresident preachers, the ups and downs of the agricultural economy, and any number of alignments with other churches as dictated from above.

Today Pfoutz Valley has ninety-some members of all ages. They use the one-room schoolhouse model for teaching the Bible to children and one-on-one mentoring to grow disciples. A choir assembles out of the congregation for four-part anthems and returns to their seats after singing. An adult organist is often accompanied by a youth on the piano. There are five active leadership committees and a quick response team of volunteers who take on building projects near and far. The altar area is often dressed with reminders of the farm and woodlands that surround the church. During the offering, so that they can give to worthy causes as their parents do, the children collect the congregation's loose change in metal pails that clang and plunk. A dozen or more elementary-aged children will have their backpacks blessed the Sunday before the school year begins. The ninety-two-year-old lifelong member smiles warmly at the sight. God is worshiped. Disciples of Jesus are being formed.

During the few weeks that I preached at the Pfoutz Valley Church, an image of remarkable resilience began to form in my mind and imagination. Here, back on slate-covered Township Road 549, was a strong community of faith, Spirit born and Spirit borne. This multigenerational people of God had outlasted the entropy of nature, the shifts in denomination regimes, and the various assaults of powers and principalities through the years.

I searched for words to name that image. Jesus' promise to Peter about the church came to mind: "the gates of Hades will not prevail against it" (Matthew 16:18). On a less eloquent note I recalled some of the colorful expressions of cussed independence I have heard coming out of the mouths of members of small membership churches like Pfoutz Valley through the years. I even toyed with adjectives from the existentialist philosophy that was the rage during my graduate school days. There is something of a *there*-ness and a *that*-ness about small membership churches that occupy space in rural, town, and city settings. They defy our neglect, puncture our preconceptions, and outlast our predictions about their demise. Mark Twain's line often occurs to me when I think about small membership churches: "the report of my demise is greatly exaggerated."

Corporate Identity

The preacher who enters a small membership church brings a call to the work, the tools for studying Scripture, and the discipline to seek a message from God for the people of God. The journey begins on a one-way street, but if the journey is to succeed, it must move quickly out onto the broader highway of two-way commerce. The preacher must become an anthropologist of the congregation to whom she or he hopes to bring good news. That congregation has a corporate identity, rituals, and artifacts that need to be uncovered and named, then respected. With eyes and ears alert, with notebook or laptop open and ready, and, most of all, with a spirit of humility, of knowing what one does not know and cannot know before asking, the preacher as anthropologist starts to observe.

One of the first things the preacher may notice is the remarkable resilience that occurred to me courtesy of the Pfoutz Valley Church. The particular small membership church to which the preacher is sent or called may have had its severe tests related to floods or fires that it has survived, pastors who disappointed, or the impact of well-intentioned but fundamentally flawed policies of the judicatory. And the church is still there.

As their preacher for a season, I may be able to build them up as measured by attendance, participation in study and action, or stewardship of the building, but the gains against their longer story are measured in inches, not miles. They really are the primary actors in a story that began long before I came and will go on, no doubt, long after I am gone.

Yet for all its resilience, the small membership church today is often shrouded in a cloud of anxiety or depression. The preacher as anthropologist will pick up hints in their self-descriptions: "I don't know how much longer we can go on." "We're just waiting for them to come in and close us." "Nobody is going to choose us when they can go to the bigger church a mile down the road."

There are other symptoms, such as the tendency toward nostalgia when talking about their church. They exchange present tense absorption in matters of worship, disciple forming, or social action for a little-brown-church-in-the-vale sentiment. At the same time (and this may sound like a contradiction) they suffer amnesia about their real history. They have forgotten the God story that gave them birth: a circuit rider with a passion for souls came into the village; a group of farm families began to gather beneath a brush arbor for revival services; the local business acted on its conviction that the town needed a house for faith. They no longer recall those Psalm 124 moments when they slid to the brink of extinction and then experienced a miraculous rescue. "If it had not been the LORD who was on our side—let Israel now say—if it had not been the LORD who was on our side..." (vv. 1-2), the fire that destroyed our building would have put an end to us, the division at the time of the denomination's merger would have swept us away; the loss of jobs in the community would have spelled our doom.

Most damaging of all, they no longer remember those instances in the past when they acted from an entrepreneurial spirit. Once upon a time they had the moxie to hand saw lumber for their first building, sew quilts to pay the preacher's salary, create a credit union for the community, serve as disaster relief headquarters after the flood, or sponsor an immigrant family. Those feats of valor are forgotten now and in their place is a resigned passivity. Many small churches today are waiting for the other shoe to drop. The preacher as student of the congregation will note this loss of corporate self-esteem and confidence over and over again. "Must find answers!" the anthropologist scribbles in the margin of her or his notes.

So here is this community of faith, resilient through the decades but showing signs of slowing down and giving up during the last couple of decades that have not been particularly kind. Zooming in past these two broad character traits, what else is there in the corporate identity of small membership churches for the preacher as anthropologist to notice? Each congregation has its individual personality, its unique corporate spirit that comes through in a hundred ways and is most especially evident in its stories, rituals, and artifacts.

In recent years students of the small membership church have tried to find the best way to capture its individual personality. One playful metaphor acknowledges the priority of lay persons to its long term welfare. The small membership church is a *house cat* who wants the owner around for the few things it cannot do for itself but who most of the time is content with its own company.

Theologians, however, offer three metaphors that plug into deeper layers of the small membership church and release a lot of energy for thought and action. They talk about its *soul,* as though there is some indelible otherness about the small membership church, a "thou" with whom I must learn to relate, not an "it" solely given over to my uses. They talk about *the angel of the church* as the term is used in the first three chapters of the book of Revelation. These angels are invisible but powerful manifestations of virtues (patient endurance, keeping the faith, serving with love) and vices (losing first love of Christ, tolerating heresy, becoming arrogant) that have congealed into a collective identity of the believers in places like Smyrna, Sardis, and Laodicea. Theologians also talk about the *voice of the congregation:* its unity in Christ as measured by the harmony it achieves or fails to achieve as it praises God through choruses and hymns, its deepest spiritual roots as registered in the fallback tunes and texts to which it retreats when under stress, and its multigenerational vitality as evident in the hospitality shown to young musicians with unfinished talents and unproven genres.

Is the soul of this congregation beaten down or buoyant? Does its angel cast a shadow from some unresolved conflict or cast the light of congeniality? Will its voice be weak and monotone or a richly textured harmony? The preacher as anthropologist does more listening than talking, more watching than performing until these questions are answered. Two expressions of the congregation's corporate identity are especially telling, its rituals and its artifacts.

17

Rituals

Rituals are any behavior with a prescribed order. A ritual can be as obvious and innocent as a child acolyte reverencing the altar or as subtle and destructive as a congregation avoiding responsible action by pouncing on a scapegoat. The preacher as anthropologist will want to study three sets of rituals in the small membership church.

There are *the rituals of communication*. Small membership churches often have firmly established networks for passing along news. The *reporter*, who attends every meeting or sits by the police scanner all day or is somehow related to everybody, picks up some piece of information and turns it over to the *broadcaster*, who moves about the community in some fashion, appearing where others naturally gather or acting as a force behind the congregation's prayer chain. It would be unwise for the preacher to write off such rituals of communication as mere gossip as critics of small churches often do. A better move would be to ask how to filter out distortions and how to harness the power of rituals of communication for intercessory prayer, pastoral care, and mobilizing ministry.

There are also *rituals of decision-making*. To the extent that a small membership church is or acts like an extended family system, identifying the relatives and the role each plays is helpful. There may be a matriarch or patriarch who must give a blessing before the congregation takes the new step. She or he may not hold any official office or even attend regularly, but the power to bless or squelch is undeniable. There may be assorted kin who gather, swap well-rehearsed speeches, and then make reasonably good decisions. The speeches are often beside the point but are essential to the outcome. There may be persons who are determined to carry family feuds into the group dynamics of church meetings, but other members who believe the church is bigger than family junk and have the force of personality to override them.

Of particular interest to the preacher are *the rituals surrounding worship and preaching* in the small membership church. Where people sit (and have sat for years) is important. Before I cajole them to come forward to hear better or scold them for not yielding their seats to visitors, I need to ask what is going on here. How does having a space of one's own provide a sense of order and orientation, especially when others occupy the seats where we may expect to see them? What scripts or responsibilities go with this pew? What saints of old have hallowed that one?

The order of worship will tell me whether persons in a small membership church are used to the revival model where everything leads up to the climax of a sermon and a closing hymn of invitation or to a more contemporary (and ancient) model of a sermon earlier in the service with various prayers, anthems, offerings, and hymns to follow as response. A time may come to challenge the preferred model, but first the preacher needs to listen well enough to gauge the depth and character of the congregation's investment in the order of worship.

Artifacts

The other major expression of the congregation's corporate identity is its artifacts. Artifacts are the material objects a congregation makes and preserves to tell its story and express its values. The largest artifact is of course the building in which the small membership church gathers, and it is worth pondering in its own right. Most small membership churches began as small groups of disciples meeting in homes. When the group grew too large for a house, it moved to a school or borrowed space from an established congregation. In time the congregation would put up its first building, always a sanctuary. Often they supplied the majority of the labor. Those forebears apparently thought that having a place to worship was enough so they seldom bought property more than a few feet beyond the outside walls of the building. When the need for table fellowship or Sunday school became as strong as the need for worship, there was only one place to add on. So they would prop up the sanctuary, or temporarily move it on rolling logs, and dig out a basement.

What does the present day building say about the small membership church it houses? What vision lies behind the exterior and its setting? What faith statements are implicit in its steeple, bell, and doors? What spirit of hospitality is written into the parking and entrance?

The next largest artifacts would be those inside the church building. There are the pews (why not chairs?), the organ and piano, the flags, the communion table, the cross, religious murals, the stained glass windows (why stained glass rather than clear?), the baptismal font, and, of course, the pulpit. There is often some worthwhile story about the origin of the pulpit in a small membership church: the source of the lumber from which it was built, the skill of the craftsman who carved it, the family crisis for which its donation was salve for a deep wound. The pulpit evokes memories of the men and women who stood there and preached. More important, it stands as a silent sentinel of the church's commitment to be a place where the Word of God is truly preached and heard.

Many smaller artifacts deserve notice as well. What is to be learned from the sign out front or the bulletin board in the vestibule? What do the toys in the nursery yield or the plates in the kitchen? What do the hymnals in the pew racks say about the congregation's voice? What do the Bibles next to them say about its biblical literacy? And above all these, what do the congregation's documents reveal about its corporate identity? Stories of heroic beginnings can be read in the flat details of church deeds. Clues to the congregation's character under fire can be found in the typically uncensored remarks found in books of minutes.

Anthropologists talk about the thick description of things—the description of things that takes into account the stories and structures that make them come alive. This is in contrast to a thin description that ignores those same stories and structures. It's the difference between an arrowhead (thick) or a pointy piece of flint (thin), between sign language (thick) or hands flailing about (thin). Many today have settled for a thin description of the small membership church. It suppresses any disconfirming data. However, the preacher who pursues thick descriptions of life in the small membership church will find a territory interesting in its own right and surely worthy of the preacher's best efforts when it comes time to preach.

3

The Preacher as Writer

The study of the Scripture in preparation for the sermon is interesting in its own right; "addictive" may be a more accurate description some weeks. The study of the congregation is endlessly interesting too. But there is a point in the week when the preacher must look up from the texts and back away from the congregation to bring the Word of God to the people of God.

Exciting new resources are available today for writing sermons. They are sensitive to the multiple forms that human intelligence can take. For example, some of us think best in words, others in pictures, some see the forest first, and others see individual trees. Other resources explore the subtleties of the creative process and the variety of methods for getting to the same end. Still others identify trends in the evolution of contemporary language and cultural sensitivities. I offer the following suggestions for the preacher as writer, not as the only way but as one way that works and as an invitation for all preachers to become more intentional about what works for them.

Wait for the Lord

After choosing a preaching text for the week, the preacher is ready to write. The first thing to admit about writing sermons is that for most of us it is hard work that must be given its due. There are legends about pulpit giants who go directly from the study to the pulpit, bypassing the writing act. There are other legends about preachers who go from the blank page to a full manuscript in one burst of Holy Spirit-induced stenography late Saturday night or even early Sunday morning.

Such legends do not help. Two overriding experiences, one personal and the other social, contradict them. First, the struggle to find words for what you are feeling or to find better words for the rough version of what you want to say is not an add-on to the process of thinking. It is that process. Until you can bring a thought into words, you cannot share that thought. It remains hidden in a land of shadows, an aspiring actress too shy to take the stage. But if you can find the right words, you can coax that actress onto the stage; your articulated thought will contribute to your command of reality and add to the goods you have to share with others.

The second overriding experience is social. Contemporary audiences are schooled in a culture of polished presentations. The rough drafts of a novel might serve as material for a literary historian and the outtakes of a movie supply a curiosity piece for the B-side of a DVD, but most of us only want to read or view the severely edited product. Perhaps the congregations of an earlier age tolerated a preacher groping to finish a thought while in the pulpit; the contemporary congregation will not.

So somewhere near the halfway mark of the total number of hours that you give to sermon preparation, the student becomes the writer. Most times the words come with a little coaxing, but there are occasions when they hide. You sit staring at the blinking cursor on a blank computer screen or the empty yellow space on the legal pad. You feel helpless, frustrated, shamed. Experience will teach you to respect these moments. Something is unfolding in your mind and spirit that will prepare the way for words to come the next time you sit down to write. It is not wasted time. Those who would bring back a word for the people of God must learn to "wait for the LORD" (Isaiah 8:17).

Many who preach in small membership churches have not attended college and seminary where they would have been coached further in matters of spelling, grammar, and writing in the active voice. Now they find themselves writing and delivering the equivalent of a three-thousand-word manuscript weekly. All who preach face the struggle with words that will not come, but these preachers face an added burden. Once they find the words, how can they present them in such a way that gross mistakes in pronunciation and grammar do not detract from the message?

One cure is to ask an English teacher from the congregation to review your preaching manuscript and sermon delivery. This weekly discipline in quality control can be combined with an annual rereading of such well-proven writer's helps as Strunk and White's *Elements of Style* or Anne Lamont's *Bird by Bird*. A second cure, only recently available, is to submit to the spelling and grammar cues written into the format of documents in contemporary computer programs. Even though they have their eccentricities, these programs level the playing field for persons who want to create a proper public document without the benefit of years of education in writing. A third cure is to remember that those who have received years of advanced education may have their own obstacles to overcome such as unlearning unhelpful technical jargon and avoiding overly complex sentences. For both groups the authenticity of the preacher and the message will buy time as they continue to address deficiencies in communication skills.

Manuscript and Memory

There is almost general agreement today that the preacher, especially the beginning preacher, needs to write a complete manuscript. At a minimum the preacher will write out the lead sentences (see below) and the wording of some of the key elements in the sermon. At the same time, there is almost universal agreement that the preacher should aim to be as free as possible from that full or partial manuscript when delivering the sermon.

Most preachers do treat the two activities, writing the manuscript and memorizing it, as discrete labors. The first is about bringing thought into words and ordering those words by some logic. It is about creating a more or less polished text that can take its place out in the world apart from him or her. The second activity moves in the opposite direction. Now, like Ezekiel, the preacher must somehow "eat this scroll" (Ezekiel 3:1) so the written word becomes one with mind, spirit, and lips.

In fact the two activities are not discrete. In writing the sermon the preacher is memorizing the sermon and preparing for a public speaking presentation with few if any notes. It is a confluence of two energies. First, there is the energy of a projection. As the preacher writes, she or he imagines the congregation to whom she or he will speak, the people of God that the preacher as a faithful shepherd can call by name and lead out (John 10:3). This image compels the preacher to search for words that are clear and moving. In the mind's eye the preacher sees their faces grow serious, cringe, laugh, light up with recognition, wince in pain, or find release as her or his words hit home.

Second, there is the energy of an argument. The preacher has fifteen to twenty minutes to persuade this congregation of something, to take them to a different place. We will look at the tools of persuasion in the next chapter, but here I want to stop and recognize the argument as the basic tool of a sermon. In Scripture, when a prophet, apostle, or scribe brings a word from the Lord the phrase "so that" is never far behind. First comes "hear the word of the Lord;" then *so that* you "remove the evil of your doings from before my eyes" (Isaiah 1:16); *so that* you "may have life, and have it abundantly" (John 10:10); *so that* you may be "steadfast, immovable, always excelling in the work of the Lord" (1 Corinthians 15:58). A sermon that meanders and rambles, a sermon that leaves the hearers scratching their heads and wondering afterward what if anything was the point, is unscriptural.

When these two energies come together in the lead sentences that make up the argument of the sermon (see below), the preacher creates a linear progression of thought that takes on a life of its own. When it is time to preach, the preacher will be able to access the whole by simply starting at the beginning and letting the narrative flow in the same way that hearing just a few notes of music can unleash an entire song in one's memory.

The Argument

The preacher will begin the writing and memorizing of the sermon by constructing an argument before the imagined congregation. The argument will have three to five movements. A *movement* is a separate direction of thought that can be supported by any number of speaking elements. The movement might be a certain experience you want to take people into: "I have never seen someone so angry." Or a certain mood you want to set: "it's your fiftieth birthday party and someone shouts, 'make a wish!'" It might be the first glimpse of a character in the text like the young shepherd David or the old prophetess Anna. Or it might name a position you are going to criticize later: "you have heard that it was said..."

A movement should be captured in a relatively short and straightforward sentence, a *lead sentence*. The preacher will spend a lot of time polishing these lead sentences. They are meant to be heard as well as read. They comprise the basic outline of the sermon. They are the necessary steps in the argument the preacher wants to make in the sermon.

The first lead sentence of the sermon, the first step in the argument, is always the hardest to find. This is not the introduction to the sermon; that will come later. This sentence will be relatively short and straightforward, but it must also be invitational. A group of fifteen, fifty, or seventy-five people have settled themselves and shifted into a posture of concentrated listening. They ask if there is any word from the Lord. With the first lead sentence, the preacher answers yes and brings the congregation into the force field of the argument he or she is about to unfold.

There are two basic options. If the preacher follows the traditional model of moving from the ancient text to contemporary application, as many lectionary preachers tend to do, she or he wants a lead sentence that shows the text mixing it up with the present time. To paraphrase an old complaint about expository preaching: you can't leave the text back in Jerusalem as you play out the first movement. There has to be some point of connection up front and a gradual movement from text to application in the rest of the movements.

Some of us surely drift away from the Shepherd out of curiosity (a sermon on Isaiah 40:6-11).

Imagine Stephen King filling in the blanks in the story of Jesus' healing of the demon-possessed man in Mark 5 (a sermon on Mark 5:1-20).

I hope you had guides like Paul, who tried to teach you how to listen deeply to the sounds in nature (a sermon on Romans 8:18-25).

If the preacher's normal practice is topical preaching, the explicit conversation with Scripture will appear later in the sermon. This time the first lead sentence needs to be invitational in a different direction. It must set the stage for the appearance of the text. That is, the lead sentence must reveal a space in the argument for the text to occupy. The lead sentence must start the movements of the sermon that will lead to the Scripture as answer sought, correction given, better explanation offered, or larger meaning added.

The harvest of our fields may be very slim pickings (a sermon on gratitude under stress with Exodus 23:14-19 as text).

The saddest four words a pastor ever hears are these: but I had hoped (a sermon on dashed hopes with Luke 24:13-27 as text).

I was nine or ten when I memorized the first great poem of my life, one about life as a purple cow (a sermon on the disciple's call to distinction with 1 Peter 2:9-10 as text).

Supporting Elements

A good lead sentence that embodies a sermon movement *wants* to draw to itself any number of *supporting elements*. Like a magnet it attracts details of description, word pictures, pithy quotes, short episodes, brief exchanges, analyses of words, humorous observations, analogies, cited evidence, and more—whatever helps to make the point. These supporting elements of a sermon are less polished than the lead sentences. Sometimes they are captured in a raw list of mostly nouns and verbs such as this cryptic version of an episode.

- Dec 23, 1998, car quit middle of CN & GA intersection, drivers in Xmas hurry, many in nice cars irritated... man in ratty car stops...

Sometimes the elements are simply noted in an abbreviated form that can be unpacked later as time permits.

- Study of birth order shows...
- Different ways people say YOU plural in different regions...
- Dr. Seuss poem green eggs and ham...
- Story of David dancing before Lord in 2 Samuel 6...
- Wittgenstein: "comes a time in every language game to shut-up and point..."

The supporting elements are the last part of the manuscript to be written out. They are kept as fluid as possible as long as possible. This is not an act of procrastination; it is an act of creativity. The preacher as writer is constantly working on the presentation of individual elements. Is there a better order of details? Better could mean an order that builds suspense or one that allows events to unfold more smoothly, or simply a more economical version. The preacher as writer is also constantly revisiting the location of individual elements. Does a particular quote need to be moved to the end of a movement to tie things together?

Have I told one too many stories in a row? Would that word study have more force if it were placed in support of another movement altogether?

The early draft of a speaker's movement with lead sentence and supporting elements might look something like this one from a sermon on worship with the text of Matthew 2:1-12, the story of the magis' journey to worship the newborn Messiah.

- *The main thing to remember about worship is not the discipline you must exercise to get there, as important as that may be.* (lead sentence)
- Quote T. S. Eliot description of magis' labor in "Journey of Magi."
- Worship interrupts our lives...can multiply worship opportunities for convenience but something has to pay...when started Sat. evening worship at Trinity...
- John Wesley called worship an "ordinance of grace" but listed it as a General Rule...how do you put those two together?... In worship God gives God's self freely, lavishly, extravagantly BUT it is up to us to get up, get our act together enough to go place ourselves in the location where that appearance by God is most likely to occur...
- Story of friend who got up early to go on boat ride to see whales...the cold, sleep deprivation, rumbling stomach, choppy sea...all worth it at whale sighting.
- Can I tell you a secret you already know? Sometimes our body leads us to worship and our mind and spirit play catchup. Maybe they show up last verse first hymn! Doesn't matter. The "maintenance" of worship is the thing.
- But as important as that discipline is, it's not most important thing about worship.

This is two to four minutes, worth of speaking material, shorter as the preacher is able to capture the exact words needed to complete the manuscript rather than reach and edit while speaking.

Armed with the cut-and-paste functions of a computer, or some older, paper equivalent, the preacher as writer keeps returning to the supporting elements of the major movements of the sermon like a tongue returning to a sore tooth. It is both a conscious writing activity in the hours closer to the preaching event and something that goes on in the back of the preacher's mind constantly. Those who preach in multiple point charges of small membership churches know that a lot of mental perfecting of the manuscript can occur after the 8:30 a.m. Sunday service on the road to the 10:00 a.m. service.

The Finished / Unfinished Product

The preacher constructs an argument, a speaking event before an imagined congregation that has direction, flow, and passion. Each sermon will have one basic argument at its heart and that argument is captured in a series of three to five lead sentences representing three to five movements of speaking in the sermon.

There are well-proven tools for shaping a persuasive sermon in the discipline of rhetoric, but those tools will not compensate for the absence of a basic movement from the "thus says the Lord" to the "so that" in the sermon. The preacher as writer and memorizer must secure the lead sentences early in the process. Sometimes the argument can be found in the logic of the text itself like the parade of characters in the parable of the good Samaritan (Luke 10:25-37). Other times the argument may be a list of positions that will be challenged in the end by some claim of the text. The text comes alive through the unfolding of an imaginary pre-text. So the lead sentences for the sermon on gratitude from Exodus 23:14-19 might look like this:

1. *The harvest from our fields may be slim pickings.*
2. *Long days of doing without may numb the human spirit.*
3. *Accidents of birth and timing may be stacked against us.*
4. *But God says, "no one shall appear before me empty-handed."*
5. *Why? Because God remembers better than we remember.*

Starting with the text or with some contemporary subject, or best of all, starting with an act of writer's imagination in which the voice of the text and the voice of contemporary experience are blended into a compatible voice speaking in the same tense, the preacher constructs the lead sentences that embody the argument of the sermon. This is a speaker's outline of the sermon.

The earlier this argument can be established, the more time there will be for lead sentences to attract supporting elements. Some of the elements (for example, quote, story, parsing of a word) will flit by in the course of creating the lead sentences. They should be snatched from oblivion with terse notes. Once in a while some supporting element may rise up and usurp the place of a lead sentence, as when a certain line begins to feel like it deserves to be a main, not subservient, point in the argument.

Good introductions and conclusions to a sermon can help and poor ones can hurt, but they remain secondary to the argument that unfolds in the sermon. In many instances the first lead sentence will serve as the first words of the sermon. If it is too jarring to accomplish that, a short observation, word picture, or background explanation will do. The point is to get into the flow of the argument as quickly as possible. In a similar way, the final supporting element in the final movement of the sermon may be the only conclusion needed, since the argument has been building throughout the sermon. But again, if it is not, a short observation, word picture, or background explanation will do. The energy of the sermon must remain in its argument.

Respecting the Creative Process

The search for the lead sentences that make up the argument of the sermon could easily occupy the first two to three hours of the eight to ten hours spent in sermon writing and memorizing. The labor is more like a poet reaching for the few right words than like a reporter at a press conference trying to capture the many. Things speed up when it is time to gather the supporting elements.

With time and practice the preacher will be able to identify this and other rhythms of the work of writing. There is a time of day when the words are more likely to come and a time when they need to lie dormant. When are those times? There are markers along the week if the manuscript is to be ready for Sunday. Where does the preacher have to be and by when in the writing process? One has certain strengths of mind at thirty but different strengths at sixty. Is the preacher making the most of the ones she or he has? There are mood swings that go along with the creative process, including a certain melancholy that is often the prelude to a burst of creativity. Is the preacher trying to cure feelings that should not be cured? There are seasons of "overtime" in the church, especially Advent through Christmas and Lent through Easter, when the speaking demands come faster and the time available for preparation shrinks. What disciplines must the preacher master to meet such times?

If the preacher would grow in such matters of self-awareness, it would be good to keep a journal dedicated to the sermon-writing life. In this journal the preacher confesses blunders, records glimpses of success, and names models of best practices. He or she is producing an account of the long journey from novice to expert. This is not a frivolous exercise in self-absorption. It is a healthy act of faith and hope. As preachers too we are "fearfully and wonderfully made" (Psalm 139:14). The God who calls us to preach sees things in us as writers of sermons—even us with our limits of nature and education—that may take years for us to appreciate.

4

The Preacher as Speaker

John Wesley is one of the best-known preachers of all time, but one of the least-known teachers of preaching. By his own meticulous records he traveled over 250,000 miles and preached 40,000 sermons in his lifetime spanning the eighteenth century (1703–91). His itinerant preaching was a major factor in the evangelical revival that started as a renewal movement in the Anglican Church and gave rise to a family of denominations around the world with a shared heritage and church governance.

Wesley left a large collection of sermons for his followers. They are dense with a Wesleyan doctrinal emphasis and exegesis for others to unpack in preaching and teaching. It is hard to get a feel for Wesley the speaker from those printed sermons. Wesley the severe editor excluded the very things that made him such a compelling speaker to his contemporaries. Gone are the stories, the passionate asides, and the homely details that gave his message a ring of truth. Contemporaries of Wesley do provide us with descriptions of Wesley the speaker. They document his unique strength of voice, his fearless character under criticism or assault, and his flair for the dramatic.

What would such an effective preacher as Wesley recommend to others who would follow in his steps? In a short address to his preachers (ordained and lay), Wesley gave some specific directions for public speaking. These "Directions Concerning Pronunciation and Gesture"[1] stand in a long tradition of education in the art of public speaking and persuasion (rhetoric) that goes back to the Greeks and Romans. The apostle Paul was educated in this tradition.

The church that lives by its preaching took up this central piece of a classical Greco-Roman education. Rhetoric became an essential discipline in the education of clergy for most of the church's history. To prepare for ministry was to acquire such skills as laying out a persuasive argument, speaking without dependence on a text, using language forcefully, projecting one's voice, registering emotions, having pulpit presence, and speaking through one's body as well as voice.

In recent decades the content of the sermon—its use of Scripture, its theology, its ability to engage the unchurched culture—and the character of the preacher have often overshadowed the rhetorical quality of the message, but the contemporary church is taking a second look at rhetoric. If the speaker cannot speak so as to be heard and understood, or speaks with some mannerism of voice or body language that is distracting to hearers, what chance does the sermon's content have, however sound it may be?

In the long tradition of rhetoric, the basic starting point is constant: a speaker of good character stands before an audience with tools like mind, voice, and body. With some allowance for changes in cultural context, Wesley's directions to the preacher as speaker are as helpful today as they were when offered in the eighteenth century. The preacher in a small membership church will find five useful disciplines in them.

Disciplines for the Preacher as Speaker

1. The Preacher as Speaker Must Maintain a Teachable Spirit

Wesley knew that most of our unhelpful speaking mannerisms are picked up at an early age. From youth we may avoid eye contact when speaking, drop our voice at the end of a sentence so as to become indistinct, routinely mispronounce certain words, overuse "ah" when at a loss for words, jingle the change in our pockets, speak in a monotone, speak without the facial and physical passion appropriate to the subject, or speak in a holier-than-thou voice. So Wesley advised persons who would answer the call to preach to work on good public speaking as early as possible, "before they have contracted any of the common imperfections or vices of speaking."[2] He knew that the longer we practice a bad habit, the harder it is to change.

Most of the lay preachers that Wesley enlisted for speaking in the Methodist movement would not have had the advantages of Wesley's formal education in rhetoric. It is likely that they would come into the ministry with their unhelpful speaking mannerisms intact. For that reason Wesley advised a lifelong humility toward one's practices of public speaking.

This humility has a creative side. The preacher as speaker needs to study the good speakers, make the effort to see and hear them, and ask what makes them so effective. How do their voices express the various movements of their message? Where do they hold their hands when they speak? How do their eyes keep everyone engaged as they speak? What facial expressions of the speaker linger after the message is delivered?

It takes humility to admit that one may have something to learn from others, especially from those younger than oneself. Wesley did not want his preachers to be passive in this exchange. They should be governed "by reason rather than example,"[3] that is, they should identify good practices and then appropriate them to fit their own person and context. They should also look for the changes in voice or gesture that arise naturally from the subject matter. Both sources of observation will fuel the preacher on the way to developing his or her own authentic preaching persona.

The preacher as speaker needs persons who will provide honest feedback. It would be beneficial to speak in front of accomplished speakers and teachers of speaking to receive their critique on a regular basis. When that is not possible, the preacher can gather a circle of friendly critics. In contemporary terms, even the smallest of small membership churches is likely to have a retired

English teacher to help with grammar and pronunciation or someone active in community theatre to coach face and body language. Closer to home, some spouses have the objectivity and timing to serve in the capacity of a friendly critic.

2. The Preacher as Speaker Must Rehearse

Wesley told preachers who had trouble pronouncing certain words to listen to those who pronounced them correctly, then read those words aloud repeatedly until they rolled off the tongue. Our starting points might be more sophisticated (for example, the podcast of a good speaker), but the technique still works. Wesley told those with weak voices to read aloud from a book for thirty minutes a day, building volume by increments, and being careful not to strain. The voice uses muscles that must be built up gradually to the work of preaching. Reading aloud can help also with voice variation and emphasis. It is a way of learning to give the drama intrinsic to certain scripture texts their due.

And then there is the use of a full-length mirror! Wesley the preacher was relentless in his attack on the human pride from which we must be saved and sanctified, but Wesley the teacher of preachers also knew that speakers must become comfortable with their speaking image, just as they must make peace with their speaking voice. Repeating the advice of the Greek orator Demosthenes, Wesley recommends time in front of "a large looking glass." Most of the work is remedial: "learn to avoid every disagreeable or unhandsome gesture."[4] Look for and correct defects of posture, such as slouching or holding one's head too high or low. Note and change the nervous "babbling of hands" or standing fixed and immovable like the trunk of a tree.

But Wesley goes beyond remedial work to recommend posing before a mirror to search for and practice effective gestures as any serious actor might. The pose that corresponds to a moment of personal testimony in the sermon, for example, is the right hand "applied gently to the breast." The contemporary speaker who stands before a mirror must search for and rehearse the gestures that will bring across the message to persons in this time and place, for example, submission indicated by open hands with palms upward or the "yes!" of the raised right fist.

In the twentieth century, the school of acting known as method acting called into question this practice of rehearsing purposeful gestures and instead directed actors to go into the core of their beings to find the authentic emotions and actions that would arise as they engage their scripts. The seeing that goes on in method acting occurs in the imagination, not in front of a mirror. By the logic of method acting, preachers would engage the sermon manuscript deeply during the time of preparation, and authentic expressions and gestures would follow automatically when they preached.

Perhaps the truth is somewhere between Wesley's use of a mirror and method acting's reliance on psychological motivation. Preachers need to find an inner resonance with their message, but preachers also need a certain conscious cultivation of body language for its potential to amplify the message, a discipline learned in front of a mirror or with the aid of a videotape, or, once more, with the help of a friendly observer. Rehearsal for preaching involves both disciplines.

Rehearsing to speak in front of others may resurrect memories of failure, echoes of harsh criticism, and issues of shame and self-worth. How dare you address your peers as one with authority? How can you possibly stand up to the scrutiny of forty adults and teenagers? Rehearsal is a time to stare down the demons of doubt by wrapping yourself in the armor of a call from God, who decided that you, even you with your less-than-splendid natural endowments and accrued credentials, are good enough material to serve as one of God's own messengers.

3. The Preacher as Speaker Must Be Audience Friendly

"The first business of a speaker is, so to speak, that he may be heard and understood with ease."[5] For Wesley whatever breaks the connection between the speaker and the listeners must be changed or eliminated. Speaking too softly or in a monotone that lulls hearers to sleep is not acceptable.

Speaking with a stained glass window voice, "an awful, solemn tone," distracts from the content of the message. Any affected tones—whether theatrical, whimsical, or whining—must be surrendered in favor of the voice we use in conversations. Body language that is "clownish" or otherwise offensive must be eliminated. Loss of eye contact is loss of connection and must be addressed. A mispronounced word calls attention to the mistake rather than the meaning; the speaker must work to get it right. Wesley recommends breaking down a troublesome word into its syllables, then repeating it aloud, starting slowly and picking up speed.

From his journals we know that Wesley worked hard to overcome a form of speaker incivility common among the well educated: use of words that listeners do not and should not be expected to understand. Everyone, including the nursing mother, the carpenter, and the government clerk, has a shoptalk that is useful in-house but not always very helpful elsewhere. When Wesley the theologian became convicted that Wesley the preacher must speak "plain," he developed the practice of reading his sermons in front of a house servant. Betty would cry "stop" when Wesley used a word she did not understand, and he would search for an acceptable substitute. The preacher as speaker must avoid the technical, esoteric, or arcane words gathered slowly through years of formal education or gathered hurriedly in intensive continuing education events for licensing or certification.

In many ways, the preacher as speaker is like an actor who wants his audience to be in the best position to receive what he is about to deliver in his performance in the play. But in the small membership church, as in many a small theatre, the cast doubles as crew. So the preacher must ask herself or himself if the environment is conducive to allowing the congregation to lose itself in the message. If not, how might she or he need to adjust the sound system or the temperature of the sanctuary? Are the lines of vision from the congregation to the pulpit clear or should she or he move the candelabras left over from the wedding held yesterday? Will the pictures she or he wants to project while speaking show well with the screen in that location? The preacher is a gracious host before beginning to speak.

4. The Preacher as Speaker Strives for Drama

For Wesley as for us the drama starts in the message of the gospel. It is dramatic that the Hebrew slaves are freed from their Egyptian captors or that God sends a prophet of hope to Israel in exile. The waiting father welcomes home the prodigal son; the tax collector for the occupying army leaves all to be a disciple. The blood of the martyrs turns out to be the seeds of the church; Gentiles like Cornelius are found to have the Spirit also; and behind them all, Jesus, who died on a cross, is risen on the third day.

As we saw above, the preacher as writer must try to capture the drama intrinsic to the gospel in the flow and argument of the message. The message must have some question to be answered, some tension to be resolved. But for Wesley, who stands in the classical tradition of rhetoric, there are tools the speaker can use to underscore and release the drama intrinsic to the text of the sermon. One fundamental discipline is to start the message in a low key and "afterward rise as the matter shall require." Short introductions in a normal and dispassionate voice range invite persons to get on board for a "warm and passionate ascent."[6]

Wesley advises speakers to borrow freely from the repertoire of tools provided by rhetoric to engage listeners. Use a clear and strong but neutral voice when you are laying out points you wish to prove, but speak with more vigor when you prove them, pausing briefly before you deliver the crucial phrase or sentence.

When you introduce another person as though they were present and speaking, try to capture something of the character of the speaker by varying your voice. When you address an absent person or object, speak louder than normal that the congregation may overhear the conversation with ease. And when you recreate a dialogue, vary your voice as if two persons were talking.

We have the advantage over Wesley's preachers in our easy access to recorded speeches and sermons that embody the tools of rhetoric that Wesley admits are best learned by observation and imitation rather than by "tedious reflections on this art." We can hear and see Adam Hamilton debate an imaginary opponent. We can study Jana Childers's recreation of a scene from everyday life and ask why it works on so many levels. We can listen and watch for the subtle ways that Martin Luther King, Jr. breaks down defenses and inspires moral vision.

5. The Preacher as Speaker Wears a Transparent Face

Most speakers probably would not give their face a second thought in the act of speaking. Surely the face comes along with the rest of the body in registering the emotions of a sermon like a well-behaved dog responds to the tug of the leash. They even may become a bit testy if you bring up the subject: "My face is what it is and it's too late to change now," or "I'm a preacher, not an actor."

And yet all of us have experienced the impact of a speaker's face, for good or for bad, on the speaker's message. There are speakers whose faces come alive to the subject that obviously consumes them. The enthusiasm registered in the speaker's face is contagious. There are speakers whose smile or frown is so genuinely aligned to their subject that we can drift in and out of listening to their words without losing our place in the narrative flow.

And on the reverse side, there are speakers whose face is more or less out of sync with their subject and the occasion. There is the speaker with a tenacious smirk who keeps using the phrase, "I'll be honest with you." Or there is the speaker whose face, as we say, "lacks affect" (in fact, a medical diagnosis), leaving us without cues as to the appropriate emotional response to the content of the message. We come away irritated. And worse case scenario, the preacher's face turns out to be a warm and persuasive public mask concealing a destructive private life that comes to the light of day as a scandal that shakes the congregation.

For John Wesley, the face is the most important facet of the body language that must align with the content of the message. "That this silent language of your face . . . may move the affections of those that see and hear you, it must be well adjusted to the subject, as well as the passion which you desire to express or excite."[7] Therefore, Wesley did not hesitate to instruct speakers on the use of the voluntary muscles of their faces. They should work to eliminate any facial poses that send out untrue messages. Wesley provided a lexicon of facial expressions for speakers to work on in front of a mirror or "a friend who will deal faithfully with you." When you speak of love or joy, let cheerfulness show in your face; when you speak of sorrow, show gloominess. Cultivate a look of "boldness mixed with respect" when speaking to your superiors. Lift your eyes upward when you speak of heavenly things.

Wesley also taught that the face is a primary vehicle through which the speaker offers or withholds hospitality. He advised speakers to cast their eyes upon hearers while "moving them from one side to the other, with an air of affection and regard; looking them decently in the face, one after another, as we do in familiar conversation. Your aspect should always be pleasant, and your looks direct."[8]

John Wesley held an ongoing debate with harsher forms of predestination theology, especially the teaching that some souls were predetermined to be saved and others predetermined to be damned. God's grace is available to all, Wesley insisted. All are invited to say yes to that grace and allow it to flourish in their lives as growth in love for God and others. Wesley's directions to preachers as speakers is consistent with his teaching on grace. No speaker is predetermined to fail and all are invited to succeed. Even those things that speakers often assume to be beyond their control, such as naturally endowed voice, mannerisms ingrained from youth, or repertoire of emotional responses, are less fixed, more malleable than they may have imagined.

5

The Preacher as Storyteller

L ooking back through the years of coming to faith and growing in faith by hearing the word preached, I find that it is
certain stories from those sermons that stay with me best.
Long after other details about the sermon like its text, title, and
worship setting have been washed away in the river of forgetful-
ness, I remember the storyteller and the gist of the story—the
sequence of events, the actors, the punch line—well enough that
I could fill in any missing pieces from my imagination and retell
those stories today.

Some of those stories made me *laugh* or *laugh at myself*. In the
laughing, moods were lifted and spells broken; there was release.
Some of those stories *enlarged my sympathies* for persons whose
context was so different from my small town context. Other stories *modeled virtue*, like the one about Lincoln choosing healing
words for the speech to commemorate the Battle of Gettysburg.
Some of the most helpful stories in this category were of very
ordinary people whose example would have been lost to oblivion
but for the alert eye of a preacher always on the lookout for stories to share with the congregation.

Some stories *led to greater self-awareness*. The preacher con-
fessed to a parental mistake and I then took a deep look into the
mirror. Some stories *located my story in some larger story*, such as
the anti-institutionalism of the Boomer generation or the privi-
leged position of white, middle class Americans.

And then there were those stories that are memorable because of the way *they provided breathing spaces during the climb.* When the argument of the sermon was getting too dense or the application was becoming too emotionally edgy the preacher told a story that provided a holding area where we the listeners could find shelter from the direct force of the sermon, collect our nerve, and then rejoin the journey.

Good stories told in the right measure and in the right places in a sermon can do all these things. They are the mementos from the messages that bring us to faith and keep us growing in faith, provided they are linked to a special set of larger stories.

The Five Meta-stories of the Bible

The core meta-stories from the Bible provide the foundation for any and all of the other stories that the preacher may summon for use in the sermon. They are (1) Creation and Fall; (2) The People of God in Exodus, Covenant, and Exile; (3) Jesus the Messiah; (4) The People of God as Gathered and Sent; and (5) The Final Victory of God.

The first task for the preacher as storyteller is to become immersed in the five meta-stories: to read and reread them in several translations with and without the help of commentaries; to ponder their vocal representations in music, their visual representations in paintings, banners, and stained glass; and to engage their imaginative representation in poetry, plays, dance, and movies. It is a discipline of saturation. "Recite them to your children and talk about them when you are at home and when you are away, when you lie down and when you rise" (Deuteronomy 6:7).

The preacher who is saturated in the meta-stories of the Bible has a repertoire of guiding images for the work of ministry and especially for the work of leading worship. One or more of the meta-stories will provide the basic theme and flow of every worship service. It will be the controlling story behind the other stories the preacher uses throughout the sermon.

Creation and Fall

In this story a personal agent, a Creator, wills the universe into existence as opposed to stories in which the universe is an accident. The Creator rescues creation from forces of chaos and sets it in irreversible time where open-ended stories can develop. The Creator takes delight in calling forth diverse and teeming forms of life and in giving them the capacity to multiply. Creation is good in its parts and "very good" all together.

Humans are meant to be in community with their Creator and each other. They are to be the stewards of God's creation, tending the earth and building life-giving cultures. These humans are given freedom of will so they might know and grow in the capacity for love. But in this garden paradise that these first humans call home there is a force of evil, one not explained, just named. The serpent tempts the first couple and they sin, bringing down upon themselves and all of creation the repercussions of their disobedience. Even so, the Creator does not back away from creation. God clothes Adam and Eve, who are now ashamed in their nakedness, and promises an end to the serpent's power to deface the goodness and beauty of creation.

The People of God in Exodus, Covenant, and Exile

God the Creator has a second project that will bring glory to God's name. God will create a people who will become a source of blessing to all the nations by going "to the land that I will show you" (Genesis 12:1-3). The story begins with the call of the elderly couple, Abraham and Sarah, and follows them and their descendents through a long journey with many tests, detours, and surprising developments. The people of God hit bottom as they suffer slavery at the hands of the Egyptians, but God hears the cry of the people and God calls Moses to lead the people out of Egypt. The Exodus of the ex-slaves is the first of two powerful metaphors for human deliverance from the powers of sin and death in the Bible.

God calls the ex-slaves to live together in a covenant community, and God makes the first move by extending steadfast love to all. God teaches the people compassion for vulnerable persons. God teaches the people how to worship and respect holy things, spaces, and times. God teaches the people where to locate the boundaries in their lives as family members, neighbors, and citizens. And God sends leaders when and how they are needed: Spirit-endowed warrior-judges when the people are struggling for national existence, a king "after [God's] own heart" (1 Samuel 13:14) when they need unity and direction, sages for their settled days as a healthy nation-state, and prophets to comfort them when they find themselves defeated by other nations and scattered in exile.

Jesus the Messiah

The second powerful metaphor for human deliverance from the powers of sin and death in the Bible is the resurrection of Jesus the Messiah on the third day after his crucifixion just outside Jerusalem. It is the end of a story that begins with Jesus' birth in the obscure but prophetically significant town of Bethlehem. The child grows and becomes strong in the favor of the Lord. For a season the young adult Jesus identifies with the itinerant ministry of John the Baptist, who calls the people to a baptism of repentance. But eventually Jesus must follow his own call, a Spirit-anointed ministry of bringing good news to the poor and release to the captives. He announces "the year of the Lord's favor" (Luke 4:18-19).

He validates the message and his role as the messenger with miracles of healing and miracles of abundance. He validates them by teaching life-giving wisdom and by telling short stories drawn from everyday life. His stories draw us in with homely details and identifiable characters but often take a surprising turn which is in fact the specific "God thing" about them. Jesus, the consummate storyteller and wonder worker, attracts crowds. With the crowds come the critics, and behind them come those who feel their power threatened by this prophet of "the year of the Lord's favor." There is a fateful showdown in Jerusalem. Late Friday afternoon on April 7, 30 C.E. it looks like Jesus' enemies here won. Jesus is crucified, dead, and buried.

But God has the last word concerning the beloved Son. Jesus is resurrected from the dead on the third day, "the faithful witness, the firstborn of the dead, and the ruler of the kings of the earth" (Revelation 1:5). He appears to the disciples, to more than 500 believers at one time, and, last but not least, to a persecutor of Christians who becomes the church's greatest missionary, the apostle Paul. The risen Lord commands the disciples to witness to his message and to him "in Jerusalem, in all Judea and Samaria, and to the ends of the earth" (Acts 1:8).

The People of God as Gathered and Sent

On the day of Pentecost the Spirit descends upon a large gathering in Jerusalem. Peter and the disciples preach in languages they had never learned. People from every nation hear that preaching about Jesus in their native tongues. It is preview of a story that will unfold across two millennia, all the continents, and hundred of cultures. The church will survive and flourish in spite of its sins, divisiveness, and heresies: one, holy, apostolic, and catholic, where the word is truly preached and the sacraments properly offered.

The story continues today. The people of God gather to worship God the Father, Son, and Holy Spirit, to hold each other accountable, to teach the faith of the apostles to the next generation, to forgive and be forgiven, and to share the Spirit's gifts for building up the body. Then the people of God scatter to be salt and light in their spheres of influence, to discern God's work in the world and give themselves to it. This breathing in and breathing out of the people of God is global, from the infant churches of Russia to the proliferating churches of Africa and South America. It is as local as the small membership church set way back in the mountains, far out on the plains, or low beneath mighty city towers.

The Final Victory of God

In the life and fate of Jesus we see a preview of what God intends for the final future: the powers of disaster, disease, sin, and death are defeated and judged. Even the memory of their impact will be "remembered no more"; God will wipe away every tear (Revelation 21:4). Creation will be delivered from its bondage (Romans 8). The redeemed of the Lord will "see face to face" and "know fully" (1 Corinthians 13:12). They will cast their credentials and achievements before the throne of Christ (Revelation 4:10) and, in the powerful imagery of Charles Wesley's poetry, they (we) will worship God forever "lost in wonder, love, and praise."

The preacher as storyteller stands at the confluence of the Bible's five meta-stories, the sermon's main argument, and a river of lesser stories that want to make their way into the sermon. These other stories flow from the preacher's memory, from the kind of leisurely pondering of everyday episodes that seems to lie behind Jesus' parables, and from the preacher's reading. The preacher as storyteller is steward of the meta-stories and all the other stories. We will look at the responsibilities of that stewardship shortly, but first we need to name a story that is too often missing in small membership churches today.

The Congregation's Story

Something like a narrative collapse is happening in many small membership churches today. The persons in those churches have forgotten, neglected, or even denied their collective story as a people of God. The last "church historian" died decades ago. Old minutes deteriorate in a damp basement corner. Elders don't pass along the story to the second and third generation. The artifacts that could jog memory lie scattered and neglected. The congregation lives radically in the present tense, but it is an act of resignation, not defiance. This church has lost its past and is fearful of the future.

If you went into one of the newer large churches, you would soon know the congregation's story. The preacher would repeat it or vignettes from it in sermons and announcements. It rolls off the tongues of members the moment a visitor shows interest. It is prominent on the home page of the church's website. It occupies space in the introduction of the church cookbook and the inside cover of the annual report. People love to tell how the church started out meeting in a funeral home, or survived the fire of 1988, or rose to the occasion of the area's loss of a major employer.

Not so in the small membership church. Why? Three conspicuous forces contribute to the narrative collapse in small membership churches today. First is the myth of endless progress that can be traced back to the eighteenth century shift in cultural perspective in Europe and America known as the Enlightenment. The past is the place of stagnation, ignorance, and oppression. With confidence in human reason and the methods of science, things can be better, and better on a larger scale. But somewhere along the line confidence gave way to obsession. What is newer, bigger, more modern must be better. The past is *only* practice for getting it right.

Second is the careless talk of mainline church leaders in response to declining membership in mainline congregations. These leaders may have good intentions, but when they speak as they do, people in small membership churches *hear* something like this: "Shame on you! You are still small! You have failed to get bigger! You are not carrying your weight! You are weighing us down! Who cares about what you once were? What have you done for us lately?"

Third is that the rapid turnover of pastoral leadership in small membership churches has taken its toll on the congregation's collective memory. The congregation is the final steward of its story, but the chief storyteller, the one who holds that story before the congregation as an act of leadership, is the preacher. The preacher just passing through, as they often are in small membership churches, barely has time to figure out whether the congregation's story is a heroic epic, tragedy, or comedy, let alone to absorb the subtleties of the main plot, the cast of characters, and the deposit of colorful details within it.

Every congregation has a story to tell. There is always a *Genesis 12 episode*, some event in the dim past like the call of Abram and Sarai to step out in faith. Some circuit rider passing through stopped long enough to preach revival. A group of believers—their offspring are present today—began to gather at the one-room schoolhouse for prayer and Bible study. The sawmill owner said he would donate land and materials for a church if the people would chose a denomination and put up the building by their own labor. They would and they did.

Every congregation has its *Psalm 124 deliverances* when "if it had not been the LORD who was on our side" they would have perished. The fires or the floods would have put an end to them. Disagreements over the merger or the new building would have become a fatal division. Loss of good givers or loss of employment in the community would have closed them. But, "we have escaped like a bird from the snare of the fowlers; the snare is broken, and we have escaped" (124:7).

Every congregation is on a trajectory through time, moving from smaller to larger, from larger to smaller and health, from larger to smaller and death; or perhaps in healthy equilibrium. The character of their journey may suggest to members of the congregation and to the resident preacher some classic plot from mythology, from children's fables, or from the Bible. We are Sisyphus never quite getting ahead. We are the little engine that could. We are Israel in exile.

Rules of Ethics, Etiquette, and Artistry for the Preacher as Storyteller

1. Honor the Meta-stories
Give them preference above all other stories. Find ways to keep them in front of the congregation. Lead the congregation in

the Apostles' Creed. Offer the church's prayers of thanksgiving over the water for baptism or over the bread and cup before the Lord's Supper. The longer prayers usually are recapitulations of one of the meta-stories. Include hymns that faithfully render the elements and the narrative progression of the meta-stories, such as Thomas Chisholm's "Great Is Thy Faithfulness" (*Creation and the Fall*), Charles A. Tindley's "Stand by Me" (*the people of God in exodus, covenant, and exile*), J. Edgar Park's "We Would See Jesus" (*Jesus the Messiah*), Mary A. Thompson's "O Zion, Haste" (*the people of God as gathered and sent*), and Natalie Sleeth's "Hymn of Promise" (*The Final Victory of God*).

At some point the preacher needs to anchor the sermon in one of the meta-stories. A recitation of a meta-story just before reading the preaching text or early in the sermon has the effect of zooming in for the sermon. Offering the meta-story toward the end of the sermon or in the closing prayer helps listeners transition back into the broader stream of worship and everyday life.

2. Honor the Congregation's Story

Honor it even if they don't! When necessary, help them retrieve the discarded pieces to reconstruct their neglected story, being especially alert to faith-based acts of courage or entrepreneurship in the past that might serve as an antidote to their resigned passivity today. Then, from time to time, repeat that story, or excerpts from it, in the sermon so those who hear may know the pleasure of participating in a local social drama. Whatever the state of their more private stories, they are players also in this unfolding version of the people of God on the way. As we will see later, telling the congregation's story is valuable also to the occasional God-seekers in worship who are not so much looking for a belief to which they can subscribe as a story in which they may belong.

3. Don't Lie!

Every storyteller has selective memory. If our story is personal, we tell it from our perspective; others present may have different stories to tell. Our purpose for using the story will determine which details from a past event we gather up and which we neglect. Time and distance distort memory. Even so, we have an obligation to remember as truthfully as we can the episodes we transport into the stories we tell in sermons. The obligation is anchored in the Ninth Commandment, "You shall not bear false witness against your neighbor" (Exodus 20:16). There is a "what God saw" account of the events behind the stories we tell. Our casting of characters, editing of script, and development of plot should not stray far from that account. Here's a helpful hint: others probably weren't *that* bad; we probably weren't *that* good.

4. Don't Steal!

Use the stories you heard or read but say where you got them. It does not break the continuity of sermon to insert little credits like "Anne Lamott tells the story of..." or "CNN carried the story..." and it shows respect for the property of others. The unsubstantiated stories flying through cyberspace and landing in e-mail, blogs, or websites are especially tempting. Often no author or source is identified; it would be it be so easy to claim them as one's own. But there is a certain tinny clink when a storyteller passes along someone else's story as if it happened to them. People in the pews hear that clink and disengage as quickly as they hang up on telemarketers.

5. Don't Break a Confidence

In a small membership church there is a lot of informal sharing of personal information: from parking lot conversations after a meeting to "Joys and Concerns" in worship, from the phone or e-mail prayer chain to the gossip exchanged at the market. It is a hothouse of information exchange, and most people in the small membership church like it that way. But, from time to time, someone in that church will want to have a private conversation with the preacher as his or her pastor. She has just learned that she is infertile. His marriage of thirty years is falling apart. A daughter just told her parents that she is a lesbian and is moving to the city. He seems to be losing his grip at work. She has been offered a promotion in a far city but has sole responsibility for her mother who is in fragile health. These persons want to confess, tell, ponder, imagine options, and just generally "get it out" with a person they can trust. Obviously, it would never do for the preacher to share from these confidential exchanges in the pulpit, even in a thinly veiled form. Less obviously, the care with which the preacher shares stories drawn from other private conversations in other churches will help set or erode the climate of trust.

6. Do No Harm to Those of Your Household

People in the pews today expect autobiography from their preachers. They want to experience the bringing of "truth through personality"[1] as the nineteenth-century pulpit giant Phillips Brooks called the process of preaching. Unless the preacher is single or spends most of his or her time alone, their stories will involve household experiences. But some family laundry ought not to be aired in public. Some PK's (preacher's kids) are at fragile stages of development where they are vulnerable to harmful shame when their lives are held up to strangers. And some spouses would beg to differ with the speaker in the pulpit on what really happened and what it did or did not prove. The preacher as storyteller should extend to those of his or her household the common courtesy he or she would extend to a bishop or moderator, an esteemed former teacher, or a close colleague who would be present at the telling of a story that might depict them in some edgy way: seek their blessing *before* using the story and then edit or delete accordingly.

7. When in Doubt, Don't!

Living with integrity is often as simple as listening to some small inner voice of doubt or owning up to the fact that you saw what you really did see. The storyteller senses something is not right. The story he or she wants to tell and the past he or she truly remembers stand too far apart. The story he or she grabbed off the

Internet has "hoax" written all over it. A little voice inside whispers to the storyteller "you really should check with Alice before you share that." Once a storyteller has rehearsed the telling of a story and fallen in love with the fantasy of the impact that story will surely have upon the congregation, imagination is likely to win out over conscience. The earlier in the process of sermon preparation that the preacher can attend to any doubts surrounding his or her stories, the better.

8. Don't Send a Story to Do an Argument's Job

The resurgence of storytelling in preaching today is not an isolated development. Across a number of fields of study as diverse as counseling and leadership, or history and scenario planning, a new appreciation for the fundamental importance of story to our well-being exists. But in those disciplines a larger conversation is always going on—a debate, an inquiry, a problem to be solved that gives stories their value, that makes them work or fit. In counseling for instance, a diagnosis of depression may require that the patient be led on a search for stories that contradict the oppressive stories they have learned from some dominant figure in the past. Story is in the service of the larger enterprise of healing.

Preaching is more than repeating stories, even the great metastories of the Bible. Preaching is a larger conversation where God addresses God's People. "Come now, let us argue it out, says the LORD" (Isaiah 1:18). Stories should be at the service of that argument: driving home a point here, providing breathing space there. They cannot substitute for the argument itself, and they will not cover a preacher's lack of sermon preparation for long. But well-placed and well-crafted stories can make a sound argument memorable.

6

The Preacher as Theologian

It would be nice if every preacher who stood before a small membership church to preach had the advantages of a formal theological education. It would be good if every preacher had been to college to take an introduction to philosophy class where he or she learned about Plato's invisible realm of ideas, Aristotle's argument for an Unmoved Mover, or Hegel's vision of universal history so that he or she would recognize these concepts when they reappear in the church's theology, as they do perennially, in recycled forms.

It would further be nice if once those persons received a college degree, they were able to continue on to do a demanding Master of Divinity program in a seminary. They would take courses in practice of ministry, like worship, preaching, and administration that would make them hungry for the study of the deeper meanings that sustain those practices in a theology of sacraments, a theology of preaching, and a theology of church leadership. At seminary, they would immerse themselves in the required prerequisites for the study of theology, such as church history, Bible, and ethics. And toward the end of their seminary education, they would take systematic theology. They would ponder the major Christian doctrines—like God as Trinity; Creation; the authority of Scripture; humanity in the image of God; universal sin;

salvation; the people of God formed through Exodus, Covenant, and Exile; Jesus the Messiah; the church gathered and sent; and eschatology, the last things.

It would be nice if, upon receiving a foundation in systematic theology, these future preachers of the church had the leisure to go deeper into particular schools of thought or subjects that spoke to their minds and hearts when they were introduced to them in earlier study: some version of liberation, feminist, womanist, or postmodern theology perhaps, or some concentration in the theology of the spirit (pneumatology) or theology of biblical stewardship. As we will see, it would be especially nice if any of these persons headed to the small membership church were to receive a strong dose of the theology of the church itself (ecclesiology).

And then it would be nice if these years of formal education were to be topped off with two to five years of preparation for ordination where the new preachers of the church received mentoring in the art of connecting the theology of their education and the everyday practice of ministry as they move from readiness for ministry to effectiveness.

It would be nice if this were the typical scenario of every preacher who stood before a small membership church to preach, but it is not. Except for the occasional ordained pastor passing through, those who preach in small membership churches have a crash course in theology in a summer or weekender school that awards a license to preach. If they are a lay speaker filling in until a licensed or ordained preacher can be found, it is likely they have never had a course in theology.

So something must give: either we say it really doesn't matter that people in small membership churches receive their preaching from persons who lack theological training or those who preach in small membership churches must equip themselves to become the theologian-in-residence at those churches. Some people today argue for the first option, as if the small membership church were some sort of haven from the doubts and heresies that plague believers in larger churches. This romantic projection is totally unfounded. The theological questions that absorbed the New Testament house churches of twenty-five to forty members can be overheard in the pastoral conversations, Bible studies, and board meetings of small membership churches today: What do certain troubling passages of the Bible really mean? Who has the authority to preach and teach? What beliefs are core and what are optional? How should we pray? What happens when we die?

The person called to bring the word of God to the people of God, therefore, has no choice but to become the theologian-in-residence. Others in the congregation may be better educated or more biblically literate, but the preacher is the one called to the work of doing theology for the sake of the integrity of the sermon. We will look at a simple three-step method for doing the work of theology, and then offer two complementary models for sharing the fruit of that labor with the congregation through preaching.

The Three R's

Dozens of methods for thinking theologically are available today, and in time the preacher may find one or another more attractive because of its starting point, the types of experience it takes into account, or the flow of its movements. The method of the three R's (Read, Retrieve, and Respond) can be thought of as a primer for those methods. It tries to name the minimum number of separate movements in the act of thinking theologically and describes the material for each movement in very broad categories. It takes hold of certain practices the preacher is already doing on a hit-and-miss basis and makes them a matter of intentional improvement.

Step One: Record Experiences That Raise Theological Questions

Stop and ponder the everyday experiences that seem to have energy to point to some larger truth. Jesus found images to describe the kingdom of God in a woman losing a valuable coin, a farmer scattering seeds, and children playing games in the marketplace. Stop and capture sights and episodes, quotes and conversations, reports and stories that beg to be set in the horizon of some larger interpretation about life. Take notes, snap a picture or video clip, copy from the book, clip from the paper.

Stop and drink in the local and national newsworthy reports that fairly scream the theological questions about the nature of evil, the stewardship of creation, and the definition of a just war. The great theological questions are not the products of the theological academy distributed to the congregation and world at large through the preacher as salesperson. They arise first in the world where persons encounter God even before they have the fullness of biblical language and church reflection on Scripture to name that encounter. The preacher only needs to bend close enough to the action to hear passionate questions about living by trust, finding purpose in life, ordering our loves, doing good and not hurting, and forgiveness and reconciliation.

Step Two: Retrieve from the Texts of the Tradition

There is a time for the preacher to step back from the action and to hold the recorded experience up to the light of the texts of the theological tradition: the Bible and the texts that help interpret the Bible. This act of retrieving from the texts is a discrete discipline that arises from the call to preach. It takes time; it takes a "study" of sorts to retreat to, and good tools; it takes discipline.

It might work like this: On the day your son receives his driving license, he borrows the family car to go impress his friends. You set curfew at 10:00 p.m., and at 10:30 p.m. the teenager is still not home. Over the next thirty minutes you imagine the worst. You begin to make bargains with God. You practice your verbal fury if your son is only being the procrastinator he often is. The child returns safely and uneventfully at 11:00 p.m., and you hurry out the front door to alternately hug and scold. Brooding on the experience sometime later, you are drawn to Jesus' story about a waiting father and a prodigal son (Luke 15:11-32). You see something about God you did not see before: how vulnerable God becomes in granting to humans the freedom to run away from God. You wonder how others might have fleshed out the subject of God's parent-like vulnerability. So you begin to trace a trajectory that runs from the Scripture to the commentaries to the theologians. Soon you find yourself immersed in rich material, some ancient, some modern, about "the God who waits" and the God who uses persuasive rather than coercive power.

Step Three: Respond as One Informed by the Texts of the Tradition

The preacher returns to the experiences that raised theological questions, only this time supplied with more imagination to unfold those experiences and with more language for connecting them to the faith of the church. The preacher does not try to impress others with the company kept during the work of retrieving from the texts of the tradition; but neither is the preacher ashamed to mention it.

In the longer view of things theology, is what Augustine called sacred wisdom (*sapientia*); it is the work of clarifying truths about God, Jesus, the Spirit, the Church, and Salvation for the sake of drawing closer to them. During the rise of the great European universities in the twelfth and thirteenth centuries, theology also began to take on the character of a science, at home with other sciences in the academy. The nineteenth and twentieth centuries were the high-water mark of this approach that called for the participant to adopt a detached, critical, and analytical posture. Theology as science has made substantial contributions to the life of the church, such as providing it with an authoritative text of the Bible in the original languages, helping it remember its history more truthfully, and educating it in the philosophical languages it needed, and still needs, to master in order to speak the gospel to its contemporaries. But theology as science also has a tendency to guard itself from interference from the church, to accumulate methods and languages that may be off-putting to those in the church, and to show a blatant disregard for the church's practices.

Before theology was an academic discipline for the few, it was sacred wisdom for the many. There is renewed appreciation in the contemporary church for the theologians and texts that help the church read its primary text of the Bible more completely: the church fathers of the first three centuries, the church giants since, and the prophetic voices of the twentieth century. The preacher as theologian will want to be borne along by this wind, will want to add to the substance of the weekly sermon by sharing the fruit of theological study. Insert a pithy quote on temptation from Martin Luther where it helps. Dare a sermon series on Wesley's threefold distinction of grace as preventing or going before, justifying, and sanctifying. Unpack Mary's Song (Luke 1:46-55) on Christmas Eve after reading a theologian who writes from the experience of African American women. End the Easter sermon on 1 Corinthians 15 with a playful recap of Augustine's speculations on the resurrection body in *City of God*.

The preacher who uses the method of the three R's or some other method for weaving together contemporary experience and the texts of the tradition, beginning and ending with the Bible, will preach sermons that promote spiritual growth. "Spiritual growth" here is not some vague inspiration that soon disappears, but a specific encounter with the Scriptures in the company of past and present teachers of the church who are there to keep those Scriptures intrusive, poignant, and productive, sharper than any two-edged sword (Hebrews 4:12).

Two major models or voices for preaching theologically exist. One is the guide along the journey of faith seeking. The second is the defender of the faith. Both are validated by the canon of Scripture, though by different parts of the canon. Both have been practiced throughout the history of the church by most preachers, with some seasons and circumstances favoring one voice over the other. Pulpit superstars can be heard in one or the other voice, and sometimes in both. Both voices are relevant to the needs of the contemporary church, but one has desperate relevance to the crisis of confidence in many small membership churches.

Guide on the Journey of Faith Seeking Understanding

One of the church's oldest and most widely held definitions of theology is that it is *faith seeking understanding*. This definition is supported by the Wisdom books of the Bible like Job, Psalms, and Proverbs, where the people of God reflect on the implications and applications of their faith. In this definition, persons come to faith first and then reflect theologically. Persons have contact with the community of faith where the preacher preaches God's purposes in sending Jesus the Messiah in the power of the Spirit. In the community of faith, persons experience worship and prayer, accountability and encouragement, the joy of exercising spiritual gifts and the camaraderie of mission. In time, persons come to confess the faith of the apostles as their faith.

Up to that point these persons have asked theological questions, especially questions about untimely deaths, the behavior of Christians, and failed life plans. But now that these persons are professed Christians, the questions begin in earnest and they are personal—not "how could God" but "how could *you*" stand there, watch, and not lift a finger to help? They are edgy, looking for a sign of God at work or wondering which path to take.

And, to keep things in perspective, many of their questions that come after the professing of faith express a healthy curiosity born in faith. These disciples of Jesus want to explore "the depth of the riches and wisdom and knowledge of God" (Romans 11:33) for the sake of a less inhibited praise of God. If "all things work together for good for those who love God" (Romans 8:28), how? "If another member of the church sins against me, how often should I forgive?" (Matthew 18:21). "How are the dead raised? With what kind of body do they come?" (1 Corinthians 15:35).

The preacher stands before the community where persons of faith seek a deeper understanding of their faith, sometimes desperately and urgently, but often carefully and slowly as if piecing together a puzzle. The preacher as theologian becomes the voice of a careful guide. Some of these persons are starting from zero, raised in unchurched homes and shaped by a secular culture to dismiss faith. For their sake, the preacher will need to be direct and redundant with the building blocks of the gospel. But the preacher will aim eventually to wean these persons from what Paul calls the baby's milk of the gospel and build their appetite for its solid food (1 Corinthians 3:2).

Other persons have become obsessed with particular readings of Scripture—Genesis as science, Paul's chauvinism, the imminent return of Jesus—to the detriment of their faith development. For their sake and for the health of the entire congregation, the preacher will preach sermons that present the whole canon of Scripture and the full complement of doctrines as named in the creeds and unpacked in the genre of systematic theology.

A third group of persons are ready now to go deeper into the knowledge of God for the sake of intensifying their experience of worship, addressing some underdeveloped habit of discipleship, or bearing more fruit of the Spirit (Galatians 5:22-23). Preachers can be especially helpful to this group by candidly retracing the steps of their own faith development in the sermon, admitting to mistaken or unfinished beliefs along the way (1 Corinthians 13:11).

Defender of the Faith

Someone must stand before the assembled people at a funeral for a young mother taken by breast cancer and speak words that help. And later that same person will have to take up the theodicy question that lingers after the loss: why does God permit bad things to happen to good people? And just as important, that person will have to dissect or deflect the crass and cocksure answers that are bound to surface from other quarters.

Someone has to respond publicly and promptly when the combined media of print, television, and Internet report the dramatic discovery of "the alarming truth" about Jesus' birth, lost years, relationship with Mary Magdalene, or remains in a burial box found near Jerusalem but fail to report on the debunking of that report the morning after by the broad consensus of church and secular scholars.

And someone has to teach the small membership church to see itself as it is seen by God and not as it is seen by many church growth gurus as a failed larger church, by some theologians as too pedestrian, by conflict managers schooled in family systems as hopelessly dysfunctional, and by some judicatory officials as a drain on the connection's resources. Someone has to teach persons in the small membership church the better language of theology—in this case, the theology of the church (ecclesiology).

Someone has to teach them to see themselves with the four images of the church found most frequently in the New Testament. They are the *People of God*; therefore, they are more than an accidental collection of individuals; they are a corporate We. They are the *Body of Christ*; therefore, they are a living organism with supernatural resilience. They are the *New Creation*; therefore, they have something to show the world about its future when God's reign is complete. And they are a *Household for Disciples*; therefore, there is gathering in, learning, and sending out.

Someone has to teach members in the small membership church that God's election of a people has nothing to do with its size or virtue but with God's grace-filled kindness and God's determination to sustain a people that will be a blessing to the nations (Deuteronomy 7:7-8).

Someone has to assure them that God has given them all the Spiritual gifts they need (1 Corinthians 1:4-9); that they are abundantly equipped to carry out their essential purposes, such as maintaining worship, forming disciples, and participating in God's redemption of the world. And more than that, in their breath-like rhythm of coming together and going out, they are participating in the very life of God the Trinity where the Father sends out the Son, the Son gathers up the lost, and the Son—in the power of the Spirit—escorts the lost home again.

Someone has to teach the small membership church a better metrics. The church has tools for self-appraisal called the marks of the church. There are four ancient marks and two that are as old as the Reformation. The marks are not a substitute for hard questions about the small membership church's vitality as an institution, but they keep the church's core values to the front when measurements are taken. They are the church's version of the official weights and measures kept by the Federal Government to guard against bogus metrics.

Someone has to teach the small membership church these marks. The church is *one*: it has unity in diversity. The church is *holy*: it is a community of moral formation. The church is *catholic*: the fullness of Christ is present in the church, and the church is able to share Christ in language understood by those to whom it witnesses. The church is *apostolic*: it is true to the apostles' teaching in its canon, creeds, prayers, and hymns. The church is where the *Word is truly preached and heard* and where the *sacraments are properly given and received*.

Someone must do all these things: answer the "my God, why?" questions, give a spirited defense for Christian hope (1 Peter 3:15), and teach the small membership church the talk-back languages of theology such as essentials, biblical images, and marks. And no one is in a better position to do that than the one who stands before the people of God to preach the word from God.

7

The Preacher as Leader

Small membership churches have a history of making do without a lot of leadership from persons outside. Many were started by laypersons gathering in homes, sometimes in response to some traveling evangelist's preaching but often by their own initiative. It might be months, years, or even decades before a gathering was large enough to build a sanctuary and call a preacher or affiliate with a denomination that would provide one. Until that point, the congregation had to fend for itself. Small membership church histories typically mention the early practice of stacking needed baptisms, weddings, and memorial services until the circuit-riding preacher came through. The blessings of the Word "truly preached" and the Lord's Supper "duly administered" had to be similarly postponed. But everything else, the regular gathering for prayer and worship, the everyday forming of disciples, and the sending out for witness and mission were lay driven and lay sustained.

Through the years most small membership churches have been subject to frequent turnover of clergy leadership. First it was circuit riders, then young persons on their way to "bigger and better things," and in recent years it is either part-time retired pastors winding down their formal ministry or student pastors staying only long enough to finish their education. Some small membership churches can list the names of forty or more pastors in the last one hundred years of their existence. Is it any wonder that many of them develop a spirit of robust self-reliance? Any wonder that they are cautious at best and suspicious at worst when the new preacher comes to town?

Some might argue that this is not a problem. They would say that terms like *leader* and *leadership* more properly belong to a corporate model of an organization, a model that belongs in larger-membership churches. They suggest that the preferred term describing a pastor in a small membership church is *friend, shepherd*, or even *lover*.

So first we must insist that small membership churches need leaders too. The people of God, regardless of size, need someone to whom they give an upward glance for the sake of orientation and direction. The body of Christ that has strong hands and swift feet needs a head to see the big picture and keep the parts working together. The Spirit's gifts that are promised to every church and to a house church first—"you are not lacking in any spiritual gift" (1 Corinthians 1:7)—includes also the gift of leadership (Romans 12:8).

There is no doubt that those who provide leadership in a small membership church must know how to lead where relationships are the prevailing currency. They must have people skills. They must know how to read terse remarks and silences. They must be relatively happy to be where they have landed. They must understand "simple" ways of doing things that can turn out to be quite sophisticated exercises in communication, wisdom, and empowerment. This is the flavor of leadership in a small membership church, but it is not a substitute for it. A time comes when the one called to it must be willing to lead, willing to stand back from the intensity and rewards of pastoral relationships to care also for the corporate life of the people of God. One must become not only a friend, shepherd, and lover but also, to use one of the New Testament's core images for a church leader, an overseer.

The evidence is empirical as well as theological. The picture of a self-sufficient organization, one able to get along without a leader, does not hold up in a careful reading or hearing of old congregation stories where a certified, licensed, or ordained church leader is clearly the catalyst who releases and focuses the native energy of a small membership church. This combination of strength to strength, leader and lay talent, is the preferred formula for moving a small membership church from mere survival to flourishing.

In 1923, from Calhoun County a wiry little man with a big voice was sent to East View.... He was Rev. A. I. Summers. Plans were soon laid for the new building.... The first service was held in the basement August 30, 1927.... There were years of debt. Some of the trustees mortgaged their homes. The Ladies Aid Society quilted quilts, put on suppers and devised many schemes to pay the debt. Rev. Summers suggested a penny drive which was a success but not adequate. Delegates returned from [annual] conference with no appropriations but with an edict that no more money making schemes be used. Rev. Summers was still the bulwark for these loyal Christians who had mortgaged their homes for the Church.... Rev. Summers served the church from 1923 to 1947. During his years at East View we have seen many dreams become realities.[1]

Rev. Richard Hartman was here the longest of all pastors. He was very active in the community as a member of the Boro fire department and EMT trainer. With his exposure to the community and his love for people, our church began to grow. He was head of the Ministerium in the area, helped establish the Food Mission, and was a good administrator for all the church activities. He also taught Bible studies and Sunday School classes.[2]

1987 brought some unfortunate times for the Wiseburg Church.... [It] was on the verge of being closed.... [P]rayers were answered when Pastor Carroll Brown arrived. Pastor "Brownie" grew both the congregation and the building.... Under Pastor Brown's direction the small church pulled together and built the annex. The church which had been struggling to survive now built space for a pastor's office, recreation room, coffee room, and two bathrooms. The ten year loan was paid off in half the amount of time.[3]

Preaching is not the only way to lead in a small membership church, but it is the most important one. Imagine a leader who gets to stand up front once a week and address the gathered people of God uninterrupted for twenty to thirty minutes. Imagine a leader whose work the rest of the week (visiting, counseling, and teaching) reinforces last Sunday's sermon and prepares the way for this Sunday's sermon. Imagine a leader whose preaching is marked by several of the consensus characteristics of good leadership, like the ability to articulate, the ability to read others, and the ability to motivate a group.

Congregations of different sizes call for different styles of overall leadership. Smaller churches require more of a chaplain or representative minister, larger churches more of a coordinator or even a chief executive officer. But preaching is one of those expressions of leadership where there is full equality of challenge and of opportunity. The basic disciplines of leadership by preaching are the same whether the preacher addresses a congregation of thirty-five or thirty-five hundred. I will list four of those disciplines, color them with small membership church hues, and suggest ways to practice for improvement.

The Preacher as Leader Reinforces the Corporate Personality of God's People

Listen to the ways people say "you" meaning the plural rather than the singular. When the Old English distinction *thou* (singular) and *you* (plural) broke down, new ways had to be invented. And so you hear such inventions as *you-all* or *y'all* (South), *youse* (Northeast and Ireland), *you-uns* (Appalachia), and *you guys* (Northern US and Canada).

Much of the Bible is addressed to that plural you, the people of God, or the church. God says to Abram and Sarai, "I will make of you a great nation, and I will bless you, and make your name great, so that you will be a blessing" (Genesis 12:2), and the change in pronouns begins. The "you" of the ancient couple (you two) starts to become the "you" of the people of God ("a great nation"). The Psalms plumb the depths of individual spirituality in the voice of the believer who stands in awe of creation, feels abandoned by God, is weighed down by sin, or has surrendered to providence. But the Psalms are also written in the corporate voice of God's people and plumb the depths of their life together from raucous praise to debilitating grief, from a corporate memory of deliverance to a corporate hope for unity. Sometimes the singular and plural voice alternate in the same psalm (for example, 44, 121) showing the presence of a multi-layered personality, one who has a sense of individuality but who is also very much a part of the community of faith.

When the prophet Isaiah says, "woe to you," when Jesus teaches disciples to pray *our* Father, or when Paul tells the Church at Corinth "Now you are the body of Christ," we are reminded that God's basic project as recorded in the Bible is to create a people, not just individual persons but a people that will be a blessing to the nations.

Whether they learned it formally or picked it up by imitation, many preachers preach as if they are trying to connect with individuals. When writing the sermon, they visualize a person or a sequence of persons to whom they are speaking. When they preach, they try for eye contact and nods of recognition. The greeting line compliment they seek above all others is, "I feel like you were talking just to me." In a small membership church the very size of the worshipping congregation lends itself to intimate preaching.

Much in Scripture validates this approach, but much in Scripture also requires the preacher to supplement it with an approach that invites persons to move beyond the singular *you* to the plural. Christian new birth and transformation are about belonging as well as believing. Even the most solitary believer must locate his or her providence in the larger story of the people of God, must move from the posture of "hear, Oh Natalie" to "hear, O Israel."

The preacher in the small membership church can reinforce the corporate identity of the congregation in three ways. The first is to plan sermon series that address the corporate identity of the congregation. Drama and application can be mined in the Old Testament accounts of God's people in the exodus, covenant, and exile. Paul's letters are addressed to congregations in all sorts of conditions from gifted to dysfunctional. And the letters to the angels of the churches in Revelation 1–3 invite the preacher to unpack not only the health of the congregation but also the mystery and substance of its corporate identity. The second way is to develop an overt expression of plural address to use when preaching: "brothers and sisters," "friends," "church," "saints," or even one of the colloquial plurals for you (you-all, youse, you-uns, you guys) as a playful way of calling attention to the distinction in hearer identity. And third, assume the preaching posture that is appropriate to addressing a group and not just an individual or a handful of intimates. There needs to be enough distance and elevation to be seen by all and not just a few up front. Eye contact is less a prolonged stare or gaze than a quick glance and sweeps. Body language is more deliberate, profuse, and hospitable to everyone present.

The Preacher as Leader Tells the Congregation's Story

If you visit one of the young and thriving megachurches that dot the American religious landscape, you will hear the story of that congregation in short order: its inconspicuous beginnings, its growing pains, and its crisis points and resolutions. You will hear that story or parts of it from greeters, from attendants at the coffee shop in the open mall outside the auditorium where worship is held, from the members of that church riding next to you in the car pool during the week. Half the enjoment of attending a megachurch is being a participant in a dramatic story that must be shared.

But most of all you will hear that story from the pulpit. In the course of a sermon, the preacher says "it reminds me of the time we . . ." or "you may recall hearing that this congregation faced a test like that the time we . . ." and the nods of recognition break out across the congregation. The preacher is the chief storyteller of the congregation's story and knows the value of telling and retelling it on the occasion when most people are gathered and receptive to a storyteller's spell, that is, the sermon.

One of the lessons megachurches have to teach churches of all sizes is the value of cherishing your church story. The lesson is especially valuable to small membership churches, where neglect of history to the point of institutional amnesia is a telling symptom of a lack of corporate self-esteem. A small membership church that cannot tell its own story is prey to a fabricated story told about it from outside by an unfriendly critic.

Every small membership church has its Genesis 12 episode: the time when God intervened in human history somehow, whether by a circuit rider, a revival, or the mother church for the sake of creating a new people to be a blessing to others. Every small membership church has its Psalm 124 litany of the times it hovered near the brink of extinction only to be pulled back from the edge. Every small membership church has a plot that is unfolding through the cooperation of disciples with divine providence.

For the sake of encouraging God's people while they ride out some menacing storm, for the sake of visitors who have reached the point in life where they are looking to surrender to stories larger than their private lives, for the sake of finding the best of a congregation's past that can serve as a foundation for the future, in short, for the sake of building up the body of Christ, the preacher must become a determined student of the congregation's history, pushing past both neglect and nostalgia. Then, in an act of strategic leadership, the preacher must tell that recovered story from the pulpit.

The Preacher as Leader Names the Elephant in the Living Room

Consider the following situation. A woman has spent most of her eighty years in the same small membership church. Her grandparents donated the property on which that church stands; her grandchildren attend when they are home for the holidays. She knows who sits in the pews and who once sat there. She can name twelve preachers back. She knows the doers from the big talkers. She keeps up with each family's sagas. She can tell you who donated most of the religious artifacts and on what occasion.

The twenty-something pastor fresh out of seminary with residues of irritating preppy talk sprinkled in her speech comes to town. And the eighty-year-old member thinks to herself, "My dear, what can you possibly teach us?" But if the young pastor has been well served by her education, and if she has the courage to follow her call to be an overseer of the congregation, the answer is, much. For one thing, she can teach them to start paying attention to the elephant in the middle of the living room; that is, those flagrant violations of the congregation's espoused core values that have been around so long that persons like the eighty-year-old member, a strong disciple on many other fronts, no longer even notices them.

What kinds of elephants show up in the living room of small membership churches? The core value may be vital worship, but the reality is that poor playing by a pianist or organist has been the overriding factor in the quality of its worship for decades. The core value may be forming disciples of Jesus, but the self-designated lead teacher of the adult Sunday school class habitually uses the occasion to bash the modern mainline church about educated clergy, ordained women, or tolerance of homosexuals. The opportunity for a life-giving encounter with the Scriptures is neglected. The core value may be to share the good news with all persons, but the reality is that first-time visitors would have a hard time finding the church, would not find parking when they arrived, and would find no accommodation for their children if they brought them.

Church leaders must keep in the forefront the congregation's pressing issues, knowing when to push harder and when to back off. They need to recognize the little games that congregations invent for avoiding the hard work of facing their pressing issues.

When they see the congregation getting bogged down in minutiae or creating an obvious scapegoat instead of taking constructive action, leaders must figure out how to cut short such games. Much of this is behind-the-scenes work, but the church leader as *preacher* can lay the foundation for this work and can reinforce it in three ways. One, the preacher as leader can preach regularly on the congregation's core values in a manner that invites the congregation to self-examination. Two, the preacher can hold up the virtue of truth-facing and truth-telling in their sermons. And three, the preacher can maintain a zone of safety in worship and preaching where the conflict over pressing issues does not reach. This last point needs some unpacking.

If a small membership church is to engage in the hard work of facing the elephant in its living room, there must be times when that church can stand back from the work and catch its breath, times when the collective attention of the congregation is focused elsewhere and upward. The preacher as leader will exercise careful stewardship over the worship, including announcements and, especially, the sermon, so they remain plowshares in the service of unity rather than swords in the service of polarization.

The Preacher as Leader Gives State of the Church Sermons

What we have in many small membership churches today are New Year's sermons focused exclusively on individual repentance and resolution; what we need are New Year's sermons that also focus on the congregation's repentance and resolution. What we have is "Form 23: State of the Church," filled out by the pastor and submitted in triplicate for the packet of reports given to the handful of people who attend the annual business meeting. What we need is a sermon by a preacher who has reflected on the congregation's ongoing story in the light of biblical accounts of God's grand project to create a people that will be a blessing to the nations. The sermon would be preached before the entire assembly, a noteworthy event with some flourish, in the tradition of Scripture where a leader assembles the people to advance the plot of their collective story as do Moses (Exodus 19:1-9), Samuel (1 Samuel 7:3-6), and Ezra (Nehemiah 8:1-12).

Most often in a small membership church the plot of the collective story will be one of maintaining a healthy equilibrium, so the state of the church sermon will answer questions like these: What honored leaders have we lost this year and who will take their place? How did we recover from storm damage to the sanctuary or adjust to the steep rise in oil costs? How will we adjust to our placement on a different charge of churches with a different rate of shared expenses? What hopeful signs are there that we will remain multigenerational? And most of all, what must we do to be faithful to our core values as we face changes and challenges in our environment in the coming year?

Some small membership churches are transitioning to larger churches, so the state of the church sermon will answer different questions: Where has our growth caused the most stress in this past year and what are we going to do about it in the coming year? Do some of our volunteer positions need to become paid and where will we find the money for those salaries? What changes in our grouping with other churches may be needed? What changes in the level of our pastoral presence may be needed? And most of all, have we been faithful to our core values in the past year even as we were swept up in the sheer activity of growth?

The hardest test for the preacher as leader giving a state of the church sermon has to be the small membership church that was once a mid-size or even a large membership church. The questions must help the congregation refocus its energy from the glory days to a less grand but good-enough future: Is our administrative structure needlessly complex and are there more economical versions we should explore? If we give up our station status as a church with its own pastor, where will lay leadership need to step up? Is it time to leave behind the much-loved but oversized building so we may be more faithful to our core values in the coming year?

Regardless of its collective plot, every small membership church must advance that plot, must take the next faithful step. With a thoughtful state of the church sermon a leader can build up corporate identity, name pressing issues, keep first things first, and encourage the congregation to take that step.

8

The Preacher as Pastor

In a small membership church, there is always one more pastoral visit to make, one more phone or e-mail message to answer, one more note of congratulations or condolence to write. This may be the case in churches of all sizes, but there are significant differences for the small membership church. The pastor in a small membership church is most likely the only person in the congregation who is formally equipped by education for the work of pastoral care and formally identified as the pastoral caregiver by office. The small membership church invites intimacy—being real with others, keeping up with one another's stories, interceding for others in prayer—and such intimacy will surface pastoral care needs. Insofar as a small membership church is family-like, it is an extended family. Those in the congregation do not forget their kin, no matter how distant in space, time, or affinity. The boundaries of pastoral care are constantly being stretched beyond the membership of the congregation. "Pastor, my uncle has a problem with alcohol; he doesn't believe in God; he's all alone; could you visit?" "Pastor, my best friend's sister just lost the child she was carrying; she doesn't go to church anywhere; could you visit?"

Given the proliferation of pastoral care demands in the small membership church, it would not be surprising if the conscientious pastor attempting to meet all those demands were to resent the change in gears required to prepare a sermon. *I was in a visitation flow. If only I didn't have to stop now!* But the pastor is also preacher. There is a time every week when pastors must stop running and glue themselves to the study desk. They must redirect their physical, emotional, and mental energy from compassionate acts of being present for individuals or families in need in order to focus on a discipline of being absent from others so they may find words to say to the gathered congregation come Sunday. It will help to remember that the two activities, pastoral care and preaching, are not so discrete after all.

Pastoral care can take place in the study and the pulpit as well as in the hospital, extended care facility, or county prison. The preacher carries the people of God in her or his heart when retiring to the study. And in that study, the preacher sees their faces and runs mental clips of their ongoing tragedies, comedies, and heroic sagas. It lends color and bite to the preacher's study of the word. In the study and then from the pulpit, the preacher attends to the pastoral needs of the congregation, their desperate search for answers to hard questions of self-worth, place in life, love and work, forgiveness and loss. The people of God want help locating the providence behind the jagged pieces of their lives. In the study and then from the pulpit the preacher will be able to address several of their desperate questions at once in the course of any given sermon. Preaching is pastoral care multiplied.

Preaching pastorally in a small membership church requires finesse and consistency. The preacher must be personal without betraying pastoral confidences or stepping on some landmine left over from a family feud. The preacher must do the homework necessary to add the personal touch when required, at a wedding, for instance, or at a funeral. The preacher must be vulnerable and candid with autobiographical stories while remembering that what counts the most is that the congregation receives help with their own stories. And more than all else, the preacher must be faithful in the weekday practices of pastoral care. The diligent shepherd builds receptivity for the preacher's preaching and buys patience for those Sundays when the sermon is less than stellar.

The Preacher as Lead Pastoral Care Giver

A reading of small membership church histories reveals that persons in those churches have been providing pastoral care for each other and their communities in the absence of a resident pastor for much of their existence. They may have begun as a prayer meeting gathered in someone's home without benefit of clergy. In time, they became an established congregation, but one served by circuit-riding preachers who showed up only occasionally and were moved to other circuits within a couple of years. Finally, they were placed in charges of multiple churches where the pastor's attention and energy were divided. And so, through the years, the disciples in small membership churches have learned by necessity to shepherd one another and those in their communities through the normal passages of life and through crisis.

This history of forced self-reliance actually places the small membership church in a favorable position to participate in two of the most important movements of the Spirit in the church in the last half-century. First, there was and is the recovery of the church's teaching on the ministry of all Christians. At least from the time of Vatican II (1962–65), there has been a growing consensus among Roman Catholics and Protestants on three points: All Christians are marked by their baptism and confession of faith for Christian ministry. The distinction between clergy and lay is not a distinction between actors and audience. In the New Testament, there were times and places when the function of ministry overshadowed any concern for office. Even when the ministerial office emerged, as it did for instance with the "bishops" and "deacons" of 1 Timothy, it never displaced the active ministry of all Christians. One clear distinction that does hold for clergy is that they are the persons especially set aside to equip the people of God for ministry and then to lead them into ministry. They are the lead or representative ministers who have received competence for ministry (2 Corinthians 3:5-6) and want the congregation to receive it. They have responded to various calls to ministry such as the ministry of reconciliation (2 Corinthians

5:18) and want every disciple in the household of disciples to answer their respective calls.

A second widespread movement of the Spirit was and is the recovery of the teaching on spiritual gifts in the life of the congregation, a fruit of the great revival of Pentecostalism at the turn of the twentieth century that reached into the Roman Catholic and mainline Protestant denominations in the 1960s. Spiritual gifts went from taboo to caution, from caution to acceptance, and from acceptance to endorsement. Spiritual gifts became the tool by which laypersons awakened to their ministry might be empowered to carry out that ministry.

The confluence of these two movements is still working itself out in the life of the church, but here and there clear changes in the way the church orders its work are surfacing and one of the clearest is in the area of pastoral care.

If the people of God are marked by baptism and confession to take up the work of ministry and mission, and if the Spirit has equipped them with gifts for compassion, encouragement, and various others "gifts of healing" (1 Corinthians 12:9), we should expect the church to be a community where pastoral care is a way of life for many disciples. It is not just the work of the paid professional. In fact, pastors who covet the role of exclusive chaplain to their congregation—a temptation in a small membership church where good pastoral care is appreciated—may be blocking the outpouring of the Spirit's gifts. They would do better, as lead caregivers, to model and teach members of the congregation who have been called to and gifted for sharing in the work of pastoral care.

Our concern here is how preaching can become the vehicle for this work of equipping. What would a lead pastoral caregiver sound like when she or he preaches? For one thing she or he will not talk like the only expert with all the correct answers but like a lifelong student in the work of caring for souls. The preacher is candid about her or his mistakes but also contagious with new learning. For another thing her or his voice is not the flat, cryptic voice of someone giving a report to a board: "I did this and this, and then I did that." It is instead the animated voice of a fellow minister perhaps three steps out ahead on the same journey toward effective pastoral care giving.

So much of pastoral care comes down to the act of a closing prayer. The issue is how shall this situation be framed as conversation with God? Should it be raw and disjointed, the inarticulate groans that only God can translate (Romans 8:26-27) or should it have intentional steps? The preacher as lead pastoral care giver already models intercessory prayer in the worship service. If he or she also will allow the congregation to overhear him or her at prayer in the stories he or she tells from the pulpit, stories garnered from his or her pastoral care, the preacher will go a long way towards to building up the confidence of God's people for their ministries.

The preacher as lead pastoral caregiver will find the resources for this work in the Bible and the long classical Christian tradition of the care of souls based on Scripture: John Chrysostom, Gregory the Great, the desert fathers and mothers, Martin Luther, Martin Bucer, John Calvin, Ignatius of Loyola, Richard Baxter, John Wesley, Jeremy Taylor, P. T. Forsyth, Eduard Thurneysen, Dietrich Bonhoeffer, Henri J. M. Nouwen, Wayne Oates, and their contemporary students, such as Thomas Oden, Roberta Bondi, and William Willimon. One example of this tradition's perennial freshness is the recent wave of renewed appreciation for the healing potential of biblical narratives. It is helpful to distinguish this tradition from the younger tradition of pastoral psychology with its attention to the individual apart from the faith community, depth psychologies, and clinical models of healing. Pastoral psychology *is* the work of specialists. The tradition of the care of souls focuses more on everyday experiences than on pathologies. It offers tools for nonspecialists as well as specialists and assumes that spiritual health for individuals is tied to their life together in the community of faith.

The Preacher as Pastor to the Corporate Body

The preacher is not the only pastoral caregiver in the congregation. All disciples are called to hear the cries of the needy that reach the ears of God the Father. All disciples are sent as Jesus the Son is sent in the power of the Spirit to announce good news to the poor, release to captives, the recovery of sight to the blind, and freedom for the oppressed because with Jesus' coming the "year of the Lord's favor" has begun (Luke 4:18-19). Some disciples may have gifts of healing that the preacher does not, but the preacher is the lead and representative pastoral care giver. The preacher draws on accumulated years of experience in concentrated pastoral care giving and on an immersion in the classical Christian tradition of the care of souls.

In a small membership church, the preacher is normally the only one authorized by ordination or license to preside over the Lord's Meal. St. Ignatius of Antioch called Holy Communion the "medicine of immortality," and so it is. But those who have presided at the giving of the bread and cup in worship and in visitation know that it is a cornucopia of healing benefits. Hungry souls "by Jesus fed" may experience such things as the sudden lifting of religious doubt, repentance of behavior, turning of some corner in convalescence, or surrender to an irreversible bodily fate. The preacher as preacher will describe these benefits from the pulpit. The preacher as teacher will equip laypersons to anticipate them when they distribute the Communion elements to homebound persons.

The most important note of distinction has yet to be named. The preacher as lead or representative pastoral caregiver stands out as the one person who attends to the pastoral care needs of the congregation as a whole. The preacher addresses the corporate soul of the congregation ("hear, oh Israel") when that soul is troubled.

The obvious occasion is when the congregation experiences a traumatic event, such as the loss of its building to fire, wind, or flood. Being present with accurate empathy is not enough; someone must give vent to the corporate emotion. The preacher summons words and images from the biblical accounts of the people of God enslaved in Egypt, wandering in the wilderness, exiled in Babylon, or persecuted under Rome. The preacher repeats God's own words of encouragement to God's people in anxious situations: "Do not be afraid, little flock" (Luke 12:32). And soon, but not too soon, the preacher leads the congregation in spotting signs of hope, shoots of new life that spring forth from the stumps of devastation.

A cloud of depression hangs over many small membership churches today that has nothing to do with natural disasters, internal conflict, or grief over the sudden exit of a much-loved pastor. These churches have lost their sense of self-worth and their confidence for action because they are under the spell of the harsh judgments of significant others. They are accused of shrinking the denomination, being quaint but out-of-date, and of having nothing of value to offer younger generations.

These churches are listless and lack affect. When a window of opportunity opens to make the worship more engaging, the shaping of disciples more effective, or some new segment of the unchurched population more accessible, they merely reach over and close the window. Resigned passivity has set in.

The preacher as lead pastoral care giver has therapeutic work to do from the pulpit. She or he must help the small membership church separate imagined fears from reality. The reality is that the small membership church is the main size of the church through all of church history, from the house churches of the New Testament to today. The reality is that one-half of the 350,000 Protestant churches in the United States today average fewer than seventy-five persons in worship. In other countries, the percentage of small churches to large is about 50 to 1. The reality is that the small membership church has shown itself to be remarkably resilient through difficult times, including the last few decades of mainline decline.

The preacher must help the small membership church find stories that counter the dominant stories of cynicism or nostalgia that are projected onto it by others. She or he will help the people of God shake off their local amnesia and look to their own collective history for signs of corporate providence, entrepreneurial spirit, and authentic witness. She or he will look to a handful of contemporary storytellers, like Anne Lamott, Richard Lischer, Samuel Freedman, and Heidi Neumark, who convey grace and discipleship in a small church setting, and she or he will lean on these writers to stretch the imagination of the congregation for living well in spite of its limits.

These preachers will summon the resources of the theology of the church to equip the people of God with better tools for church evaluation than those they may have picked up accidentally elsewhere, from impertinent church growth critics, for example, or from impatient judicatory officials. They will season their sermons with the church's God-given metrics of *essential tasks*, *true marks*, and *scriptural names*. From time to time—the Sundays following Pentecost is an obvious choice—they will unpack one of these tools of measurement, allowing its arguments, imagery, and related stories to saturate the corporate soul of the congregation.

One of the pleasures of pastoral care is to watch a healing take place. The pastor sees the difference that a week of convalescence, a month of physical therapy, or a season of marriage counseling can make. The pastor is humbled in the presence of healing powers from God, from human agents, and from the created order itself. It is good to be a participant in the healing process. That pleasure is multiplied tenfold when the patient is the corporate congregation restored to robust health and finding new confidence for worship, disciple making, and social holiness.

9

The Preacher as Prophet

L et us start with the assumption that a preacher must possess both the voice of a pastor and the voice of a prophet and that this holds true whether that preacher is in a small membership church or a church of any other size. A given preacher may be more comfortable with one voice or the other. Some are strong in gifts of mercy and service, others in gifts of discernment and speaking the truth.

Whether one is more comfortable in the role of pastor or in the role of prophet does not finally matter. What matters is that the canon of Scripture includes and forever will include both pastoral books, like Psalms and the Letters to Timothy, and prophetic books, such as Isaiah, Hosea, and Revelation. What matters is that the threefold office of Jesus Christ (prophet, priest, and king) models a minimum diversity for the office of preaching. What matters is that the list of core values for the vast majority of Christian churches specifies both personal and social transformation.

Glimpses of the Small Membership Church

To this inescapable mandate to hold together the pastoral and prophetic voices in preaching we must add one more stubborn fact of life in the small membership church: the saints and the sinners, the owners and the workers, the Democrats and the Republicans often are packed together in incredibly tight quarters! Consider these scenarios taken from small membership churches.

Self-quarantined in a Community of Moral Formation

Two couples in the same congregation dissolve their marriages. Much finger pointing follows but no clear innocents or villains emerge. The husband of the first couple marries the wife of the second. The wife of the first couple marries a widower from the same congregation. The husband of the second couple marries a much younger divorcee with three children. All of them continue to attend the same worship, want the pastor to officiate at their second weddings, and find ways to show deference to their former spouses while negotiating care for the children.

This is not a melodramatic reality TV show. This is a small membership church where persons' need to belong to a community outweighs their discomfort at being in the presence of persons from whom they are now estranged. They are self-quarantined in a community of formation where disciples of Jesus must learn to repent, forgive, and remember no more.

The Peach Orchard from Both Sides

The owner of peach orchards exits his three-story manor house with five bedrooms, 5.5 bathrooms, and white columns in front, gets into his fully equipped SUV, and drives to the little wooden church built on property donated by his grandparents. The church connects him to memories of a happy past. The couple that works as laborers in those same orchards exits their one-story cinderblock house on Sunday morning. They pile themselves and their five children into a beat-up, four-cylinder economy car with a headlight held in place by duct tape and head for the same place. The church connects them to hopes for a better future.

In the worship service, there is an uneasy stiffness at the passing of the peace between employer and employee. One of them finds the praise choruses too fast and loud, the other finds the hymns too slow and hard to understand. Some Sundays, the peach orchard owner thinks, "I don't belong here anymore; things have changed too much." Some Sundays, the peach orchard workers think, "We don't belong here; what were we thinking?" Yet all will return next Sunday and peel away another layer of stereotype to get at the child of God beneath. And the little congregation continues to wobble toward a unity in Christ that overcomes the severe and instinctive barriers of social status. In its imperfect but good-enough way the congregation previews the final reign of God, where the "first will be last, and the last will be first" (Mark 10:31).

The Strike and Other Scripts

The teachers and school board members in a small rural town are sharply divided over a new teacher contract. The teachers are talking strike. The school board members are talking permanent replacements. At some congregations, one side or the other, one perspective or the other, clearly dominate; but in the small membership Baptist church on the edge of town, both groups and both sides of the argument are well represented.

Both sides have learned to check their inflamed rhetoric at the doors of the church. They know they are caught up in a script and that it is too late to change their designated parts, but they realize that, in the church, God calls them to better parts in higher scripts. They sing God's praises with symbolic harmony. They pass the peace without calculation. And they pray passionately for the next person from either side facing prostate cancer, loss of an aging parent, or concern for a prodigal child.

The Making of a Prophet

A preacher with an authentic prophetic voice is at the heart of each of these scenarios, someone who will exercise a pastoral office and a prophetic office simultaneously in a small membership church where the Spirit of Jesus Christ seems to take delight in holding together a diverse cast of characters in close quarters.

The respective preachers in the above scenarios came equipped for the moment. Each had self-awareness about his or her social location and the difference it makes in a person's view of things. Two of those preachers started out life relatively poor, rose through the education required for ordination, but did not forget their roots. The other came from an upper-class family where privilege was more a call to public service than an election to private pampering. The three were good at reading cues and speaking across class and culture.

To self-awareness add formation. Each was educated and equipped for ministry in a denomination that recognizes the full canon of the Bible, the three offices of Jesus Christ, and a set of core values that holds together individual and social transformation. For one, the prophetic voice came naturally, so much so that he had to work at toning down the bluntness of his speech and the specificity of his illustrations. He learned the hard way that prophetic speech that drives people away yields a hollow victory. The other two preachers had the opposite challenge. Preparing to speak a prophetic word was a traumatic experience for them. They imagined worst-case repercussions. They sought the cover of a thousand qualifications. They lost sleep the night before preaching. But in the end they were faithful to the prophetic message.

To self-awareness and formation add social awareness. All three were aware that all but a handful of the churches in the mainline denominations to which they belong had become so comfortably middle-class and upper-middle-class that it was now hard for them to offer hospitality to other classes or ethnic groups. These three preachers knew they were preaching to congregations that were less diverse, economically and otherwise, than they would have been a hundred, or even fifty, years ago. Could the doors of hospitality be opened again?

Forth-telling and Foretelling

In the Bible, prophets both forth-tell and foretell. They tell forth things that must be said even if it will be hard for others to hear and they cast visions of judgment or deliverance, even when others are oblivious to the signs. When the prophetic voice is absent or silenced, Israel and the church are in moral and spiritual jeopardy. And it is a sure sign of God's continuing investment in God's people that God continues to send prophets to the people.

When the Hebrews are so dispirited that all are ready to abandon the community project and go their separate ways, God sends Samuel to pull them together. When a leader of the people, David, becomes caught in a downward cycle of sin, God sends Nathan to break the spell. In Israel's days of opulence and arrogance, God sends Isaiah; in days of exile and despair, God sends Jeremiah. God sends the prophet Anna to help the people of God seize the moment of the Messiah's coming. Other women prophets help the church at Corinth understand "all mysteries and all knowledge" (1 Corinthians 13:2). And God cares for the ongoing health of the house churches of the New Testament by pouring out spiritual gifts for prophecy.

God cares too much for the small membership church of our time to sit idly by and let it become a silly caricature of its former self. God remembers those churches as vibrant communities of faith where persons held each other accountable, told each other the truth in love, and had a fierce determination to be a light against the surrounding darkness. God remembers those churches as resilient communities of hope where young imaginations were ignited by the Bible's stories and old imaginations found visions for transcending despair.

God remembers the better self that the small membership church may have forgotten. So God sends the preacher as prophet to awaken the slumbering spirit. It is difficult and delicate work in a setting of high visibility. No wonder that many preachers in small membership churches prefer to see themselves

89

as pastoral first, last, and only. I offer the following suggestions to those who understand that the prophetic voice is not optional, though it is often uncomfortable. I offer them for the sake of promoting effectiveness in prophetic preaching and avoiding unnecessary conflict.

Forth-telling in a Small Membership Church

1. Preach Necessary Truth but Protect Confidences

In a small membership church, a lot of informal sharing of personal information goes on: at parking lot meetings after the church meeting, through phone or e-mail prayer chains, in gossip exchanged at the market. The small membership church is a hothouse of information exchange, and many members like it that way. But, as we've mentioned earlier, from time to time someone will want to have a private conversation with the preacher as their pastor. They want to confess, tell, ponder options, and just generally "get it out" with a person they can trust.

It would never do for the preacher to share from these confidential exchanges in the pulpit, even in a thinly veiled form. In the first scenario above, *Self-quarantined in a Community of Moral Formation*, the preacher could preach boldly and productively on the church as unfaithful spouse from Hosea or God's intention for marriage from Ephesians 5 because she understood the tonal difference between being relevant and being intrusive.

2. Preach Necessary Truth but Stay Connected

The preacher in *The Strike and Other Scripts* was one of a handful of persons in the school district who was trusted by both sides of the teacher contract dispute. He worked very hard to keep it that way: distributing his weekday visits evenly, checking and double-checking what he thought he heard, and reframing one side's harsh messages to the other before delivering them. If Sunday's sermon would have obvious application to the dispute, and if it would seem to come down harder on one side, the preacher would visit a leader or two of that side, alert them to what was coming, and share from the heart how he hoped his words would be taken.

These pre-sermon visits were some of the worst and best visits of his ministry. They often got stuck in the mud of well-worn arguments, with the parishioner refusing the courtesy the preacher intended. But occasionally a parishioner was able to appreciate that he was not an agent of the other side but of God, whose thoughts are higher than our thoughts (Isaiah 55:9).

3. Preach Necessary Truth but Allow Space for Persons to Come to Their Senses

The preacher from *The Peach Orchard from Both Sides* burned with anger at some of the practices of those in power but knew the futility of blunt confrontation. He was schooled in the wisdom of the prophet Nathan. By the time the Lord sent Nathan to confront David, the fallen king, David was brazen in his sins, caught in a downward spiral of dereliction of duty, adultery, lies, murder, and cover-up (2 Samuel 11). A direct accusation could have been disastrous, hardening David's heart and shortening Nathan's life. So the prophet tells a story about a poor man who worked for a rich man. The poor man had a much-loved pet, a ewe lamb. One day the rich man entertained a traveler by taking the poor man's lamb rather than killing one of his own. David is indignant, an emotional response with which he had been out of touch lately. "As the LORD lives, the man who has done this deserves to die." Nathan then can say, "You are the man!" (2 Samuel 12:5-7). And David's moral reformation begins.

This preacher found the parables of Jesus especially helpful. They allowed workers and owners to "hear and not hear." The parables tapped into work cycles familiar to both: sewing, pruning, and harvesting. They lifted the unique experiences of one group to the attention of the other: workers waiting in the marketplace to be hired for the day, an owner's impatience with an unfruitful tree, workers' long hours when the crop is ripe, and an owner's pain with a rebellious child. And the parables became an encounter with God for all. Although a low-grade tension born in class consciousness never quite went away, both the workers and the owners found overriding reasons to hold together as a community of faith.

Foretelling in a Small Membership Church

1. Foretell Judgment but Let It Be God's Judgment

Many small membership churches may be headed for extinction. In the narrative history of many churches, you will find a line like this: "Then in 1909, the band mill closed. The dimension mill then closed. Following World War I, the post office, the freight station and grist mill closed."[1] The loss of larger community vitality, whether that community is a city ward or a rural route, is a fact of life for many small membership churches. The membership is dwindling to a precious few and the precious few are getting very tired.

The preacher called by or appointed to such a congregation may feel the need to hold out the threat of a discontinued people and an abandoned building. The signs of God's judgment are unmistakable. But are they? If the small membership church has failed repeatedly to perform its essential tasks, live up to the marks of the true church, or respect its corporate providence, its present condition may be in fact a judgment from God. The preacher as prophet should summon the courage to say so as well as to specify acts of corporate repentance. But some developments in small membership churches have nothing to do with signs of God's disfavor. They are simply one generation's preference for large, anonymous localities, for instance, or the rising cost of health insurance for full-time clergy. The role of the preacher as prophet in this situation is to counsel flexibility, resilience, and hope for things unseen.

The rest of the story of Orlena United Methodist Church as told in 2007:

> Then in 1909, the band mill closed. The dimension mill then closed. Following World War I, the post office, the freight station and grist mill closed. . . . A strong work ethic, spirit, prayer and music carried them through. . . . Over the next 55 years, there seemed to be one or two families willing to do whatever it took . . . and God was worshipped through good times and bad. . . . A new Corridor Highway System is under construction. The first exit is Gilman. The first church off that exit is Orlena UMC.[2]

2. Foretell the Beloved Community but Don't Overlook the Clues in Family Systems

A favorite expression of dismissal for a small membership church is that it is "nothing but a family chapel." One grain of truth behind this charge is that often there is a dominant family in a small membership church; often they are descendents of one of the founding families. Another grain of truth is that sometimes that family is a closed society that wants to perpetuate its exclusive hold on power. Those who analyze unhealthy churches hovering near death call this the "aristocratic" symptom.

But families can be healthy as well as sick. They can be hospitable and generous as well as anxious and closed. So I want to name an audacious fact somehow overlooked by many outside observers of small membership churches: the closest thing to the New Testament church that many of us have ever seen is some form of a "family chapel" at work. It starts with a healthy family or two. Members of these families support one another in good times and bad, encourage individual development, cherish memories, celebrate holidays, bless marriages, welcome new babies, and commend those who pass to the everlasting arms of God. These families tend to adopt other persons of the congregation into generous and ever-expanding and entwining circles of love.

Some of the most compelling previews of the beloved community are close at hand in the small membership church. An adult brother helps a cousin out of debt. A woman opens her home to a runaway teenage niece who is pregnant. A family keeps contact with an alcoholic, imprisoned, or senile uncle. These quiet acts of love set a high standard for faith with works in the Body of Christ. At a minimum the preacher as prophet will want to declare, "The kingdom of God has come near to you" (Luke 10:9), search for similar vignettes and stories outside the life of the congregation, and use them discreetly in sermons. As we will see later, the preacher as evangelist might want to push the envelope considerably farther.

3. Foretell, Just Foretell

All three of these preachers from these stories had one more thing going for them that set them apart as effective prophets preaching in small membership churches. They were incurable optimists, one by native personality, two by overcoming early obstacles, all three by spiritual formation and theological equipping. They believed their congregations' best days were ahead, not behind. And they were determined to stay long enough to complete major acts of transformation in their congregations rather than seek new appointments as soon as they encountered resistance.

Many small membership churches are caught in an interminable present tense. They cannot recall their past acts of entrepreneurial spirit. They dread the future and are waiting for some other shoe to drop. They desperately need preachers who will foretell. They need preachers who will imagine with them amateur improvements of building, ministry, and mission. They need preachers who will paint verbal pictures of healthier *but not dramatically larger* congregations twenty years down the road. And they need preachers who will receive from God and share with God's people timely symbols of hope in the spirit of Jeremiah purchasing land on the eve of exile.

The Preacher as Evangelist

These are the sorts of collective memories of the preacher as evangelist that haunt the average small membership church today.

[From the 1800s] It was during this time that there was a great revival under Dr. A. P. Hyde. Miss Edith Miller (1872–1955) recalled hearing his sermon on "The Valley of Dry Bones" and the great spirit of revival and the many conversions that took place as a result.[1]

[From the 1900s] During the pastorate of Rev. Benjamin L. Moore, 1904–1908, a large revival was experienced and there were approximately 100 converts.[2]

[From the 1950s] The congregation kept growing, and in 1954, after a five-week revival, where there were 87 conversions, it was apparent that a larger church was needed.[3]

The small membership church revival services of the 1800s, the 1900s, and even up to the 1950s had a lot going for them. They were social events packed with high drama and emotional release. They helped ward off rural isolation and urban anonymity. They were gala events of inspirational music: solos, gospel quartets, orchestras, and four-part singing by the congregation showcasing the work of revival hymn writers across two centuries like Charles Wesley, Fanny J. Crosby, and Charles A. Tindley. They were spurred on by the highly publicized best practices of superstars like Dwight L. Moody, preacher, and Ira D. Stankey, singer, in one generation, or their counterparts in other generations.

At the center of these revival meetings, a preacher spoke of ultimate things like a lawyer arguing passionately in front of a jury that must render a verdict. Even in the smallest of small membership churches, that preacher could assume three things. First, the social environment favored what the preacher was doing; that is, factors like rural isolation and urban anonymity that made a revival work elsewhere would make it work locally. Second, persons who stood outside the Christian faith were present. The hoi polloi,[4] the crowds in the Gospels who are drawn to Jesus' words and deeds of power but maintain a safe distance, were present. The congregation would be a healthy mix of insiders and outsiders. Third, in the course of the revival meeting, some of the outsiders would respond to the altar call. They would repent, accept Jesus as Savior, and begin to walk by faith. Sooner or later that walk would lead them into the community of faith. The small membership church would grow by the addition of such persons.

None of these assumptions hold today. Private and public transportation, phones, cell phones, The Internet, and a staggering array of devices for home entertainment offer alternative, if more expensive ways to address rural isolation and urban anonymity. It is easier and more entertaining to sit in the comfort of one's home in front of a forty-two-inch plasma screen television and watch T. D. Jakes than to go out to the local small membership church and sit through a shabby imitation.

The crowds of the Gospels, the outside but curious onlookers, are no longer present. Small membership churches were once at the center of community life. Their modest buildings housed worship and Sabbath schools on Sunday and doubled during the week as public school classrooms, township meeting space, and food and clothing distribution centers. The social interaction between members of those churches and other persons in the community was natural and easy. The boundary between outsiders and insiders was fluid. But now the center of community life has moved to the nearby superstore. Church buildings sit empty except for Sunday morning, when a shrinking group of older persons gather to worship. That group is becoming more fixed in its habits of church life and, therefore, more odd to those outside the church. The boundary between church members and the younger, more diverse population moving into the area has become well defined, even intimidating.

And all this means that if and when that church holds an annual revival, and if and when the preacher as evangelist offers an altar call hoping for the successes of yesteryear, it is usually a disappointing occasion all around. "No one was saved!" The best slant on it is that the small membership church does a good job at growing the disciples it already has; therefore, it is okay that the revival service turned out to be an essentially in-house activity. A less positive but more truthful verdict is that the revival that fell flat is one more indicator that the small membership church is not what it used to be.

We must find a new and more effective model for the preacher as evangelist in the small membership church. Here too nostalgia is the enemy of the small membership church. The memories of the revivals of the 1800s, the 1900s, and the 1950s that haunt older members and pastors of small membership churches have become a handicap. Alternative stories must be sought. A new model of the pastor as evangelist, one that takes into account the changed social location of the small membership church, is needed.

Hard Facts and Theological Help

Some of the hardest of hard facts about small membership churches today are these:

1. *They are no longer at the center of their communities.*
2. *The boundaries between insiders and outsiders have grown*

more pronounced, and it is not because members inside have determined to become a counterculture in the best sense of Romans 12:1-2.

3. It is hard to get outsiders interested in the esoteric activities of a congregation when they have such easy access to so many other interesting groups.

4. There are very few visitors present in small membership church worship services; the crowds are missing.

5. People who join small membership churches almost always join because of an influential relationship that leads to other relationships.

6. People almost never join a small membership church when they come as autonomous individuals to an impersonal setting where an evangelist makes such a compelling case for their need of salvation that they break down in front of a crowd of strangers and make a radical change in commitment.

The theological help this time comes from church history with its memory of a more ancient sequence of evangelism than the one bequeathed to small membership churches by frontier revivalism. In frontier revivalism, the order was this: *First, you change belief.* In a social gathering a preacher makes a passionate case, and you respond to an invitation to make an explicit decision after hearing the evidence. *Second, you change behavior.* You allow the change in belief to begin to work itself out in your life (sanctification). For example, you forsake the works of the flesh and aspire to the fruit of the Spirit. *Third, you change belonging.* Almost as an afterthought or instance of the second step, you seek out and affiliate with a community of faith where you will be "fed by the Word" and begin to enjoy Christian fellowship.

But in the ancient house churches and most of the smaller churches throughout two millennia of history, the sequence is reversed. *First, you change belonging.* Perhaps timidly, perhaps dragging your protective armor with you, you begin to participate in a community of faith. You do it out of curiosity. You do it out of boredom. You do it out of a terrible loneliness. You do it because you realize your private story is no longer enough and you want to give yourself over to a larger collective story.

Second, you change behavior. You are welcomed into the family and you begin to take on the family's traits in a more or less subtle process of assimilation. There are models and there are mentors. There are vices to be outgrown and virtues to be acquired. You begin to master the things that "go without saying" in a community of faith. *Third, you change belief.* The word preached, taught, witnessed, sung, discussed, debated, remembered, and reflected upon does its good work. You grow into the ancient faith handed down from the apostles and confess it with ever greater degrees of confidence and articulation—a process of formation called catechesis. You become a witness to that faith.

Today churches of all sizes, and especially new churches starting up, are finding wisdom in this ancient sequence of evangelism. It seems especially relevant to small membership churches because it plays into what has always been their greatest strength, the intimacy of a community of faith where persons can be known by name and story, where quiet expectations of participation run high, and where accountability and encouragement flow naturally.

It also a warning to those churches: their capacity to fulfill the mandate of the risen Lord, "Go therefore and make disciples of all nations" (Matthew 28:19), begins with the health of the faith community. Has a small membership church become a closed club with secret codes? Has the dominance of one family or group become a hindrance? Is some family feud spilling over into its social dynamics? Has financial strain robbed it of all pleasure in ministry and mission? If the first step to becoming an articulate disciple of Jesus Christ is a change in belonging, the first work of the small membership church is to make sure the first step is easy to take.

And how does the preacher as evangelist fit into this ancient/modern sequence of evangelism so dependent on the health of the faith community? Even though gifts for charismatic speaking, defending the faith, and leading persons to make life-changing decisions count, it is clear today that they are not enough. There cannot be "many," "87," or "100" conversions as mentioned above if the preacher is preaching only to the choir. The preacher cannot ignore the attraction of the faith community in making new disciples for Jesus Christ and in fact must include the constant shaping of that community in the work of evangelism. With that in mind I want to suggest three contemporary images of the preacher as evangelist to supplant the image of the revival speaker.

The Preacher as Importunate Host

Jesus told a parable about a man who gave a great dinner party (Luke 14:15-24; Matthew 22:1-14). He sends out his slave with an invitation but receives nothing but excuses and regrets. Jesus says the man is angry but will not be frustrated. So he orders his slave to "go out at once into the streets and lanes of the town and bring in the poor, the crippled, the blind, and the lame" (Luke 14:21). The slave reissues the invitation and this time receives a much better response. He reports that there is still some space available. "Go out into the roads and lanes," his master tells the slave, "and compel people to come in, so that my house may be filled (v. 23).

This importunate host reminds us that Jesus' ministry began in a hometown synagogue, approached those educated by Torah to look for the Messiah, and reached out to those connected to the Temple establishment. It reminds us that Jesus' invitation also encountered excuses and regrets, not to mention outright resistance. But most of all it reminds us that Jesus would not be frustrated. He reissues the invitation with better results, and the "sinners," the infirm, and the outcasts receive him gladly. The house is filled and the party can begin.

Imagine the preacher as importunate host determined that the house be filled with *somebody*! The preacher transmits her or his passion to others in the congregation by preaching from the

Bible's rich deposit of texts on hospitality. She or he embodies the good host in worship by avoiding shoptalk and explaining the open communion table. The preacher consciously engages more than one generation in her or his sermons.

But imagine going one step further. Imagine the preacher seeking and then exploiting opportunities to "take the show on the road," that is, timely openings for the congregation to practice some aspect of its life together outside the walls of the church building. The preacher as evangelist directs the congregation as street performer in corporate acts of praying, witnessing, and working in Jesus' name in the most desperately needy nook of the county, or block of the city, or anywhere in the bustle of everyday life, being church without walls wherever crowds gather.

The Preacher as a Two-way Translator

The boundary between those inside small membership churches and those outside has become more fixed and impenetrable. It has become all too easy for those inside to stereotype those outside with labels like "secular," "post-Christian," and "the Me generation." It has become all too easy for those outside small membership churches to stereotype those inside with labels like "quaint," "family chapel," and "antique."

The preacher as leader knows that the health of any organization depends on its ability to draw nourishment from its surrounding environment. An organization cut off from its environment for prolonged periods of time will die. The preacher as evangelist can determine to do something about this by engaging in the hard work of two-way translation. Translation in one direction is hard enough! It takes concentrated listening. It takes a diligent searching for the right words to convey intended meaning. It takes watching to see if a given translation works and quickly revising when it does not. Two-way translation, the kind we see at diplomatic summits, hostage negotiations, and labor disputes, is double the work and rightly prized by all parties involved.

Carefully, persistently, the preacher translates the church's message for visitors. He or she does not assume that those visitors are familiar with the vocabulary of Christian faith. He or she does not assume that the outside world has equipped them with biblical literacy. If the preacher has been at the work of preaching for a couple of decades, the preacher may discover that these days he or she is often reverting to a more elementary level of language, one that more nearly reflects the reading level of the general public and is more likely to connect with those outside the church. But the preacher will not rest there; forming disciples is a matter of language. It always involves greater immersion in the words of Scripture, growth in the core doctrines of the apostolic faith, and refining the language of praise, prayer, and witness.

Carefully, persistently, the preacher translates the crowds to those inside the small membership church. She or he does this by acquaintance intensified by study. "Who in the world are they out there," the preacher asks, "and what do we have to offer them?" The preacher studies demographic statistics. She or he studies portraits of the generations and reads contemporary novels, movies, newspapers, and web pages. And the preacher asks how God the Spirit might be wooing persons back to God and what part the small membership church might play in that unfolding drama of their salvation. In sermons she or he is defining external reality for the small membership church, and it is a reality of real people, not stereotypes.

The Preacher as Coach of Lay Witness

If belonging comes before behaving and believing, hospitality to those outside is the small membership church's first order of business. But once the guests have arrived and are comfortably seated, then what? In the revival model, the preacher as evangelist would take it from there, sharing good news with more or less personal transparency. But this model contradicts the most important fact of small membership church life: members of the congregation are more important to its vitality than the preacher.

Every preacher today must work toward a healthy transparency in preaching, sharing things personal but not private in the service of the gospel. People are hungry for contemporary models of discipleship. They want to hear about the vulnerability, mistakes, and struggles as well as about the victories and growth. They know God's grace is foremost in the end but they want to explore the nuances of human response to that grace along the way. The preacher will find it helpful to consider the example of Paul who, without embarrassment or hypocrisy, could advise persons in the churches to whom he ministered, to "imitate me" (1 Corinthians 4:16, 11:1; Philippians 3:17, 4:9; 1 Thessalonians 1:6).

But in the small membership church it cannot end there. The preacher who practices transparency in the pulpit must push the envelope of corporate transparency, must enable the people of God to tell their own stories of amazing grace. The preacher already knows that such stories exist in the same way he or she knows that there are compelling vignettes of the beloved community lodged in the family systems of the congregation. There are sermons where one or more of these stories would be the perfect fit, but to protect the boundaries of pastoral confidentiality and to guard against suspicions of preferential treatment, the preacher may refrain from using them at this time. Instead, he or she hoards them for eulogies or for preaching at the next church.

Suppose the preacher as evangelist were to take it upon herself or himself to coach persons in the work of sharing their stories of grace and their vignettes of beloved community in the worship service? Unlearning is a good part of it. For as far back as anyone can remember, laypersons only stood before the congregations to give *announcements*, to explain, wheedle, cajole, load with guilt, and say the same thing six different ways. But before laypersons were drafted as cheerleaders for the institution, they were witnesses rising to tell the assembly what God had done in their lives.

The preacher who will take the time to coach persons to speak up, use first person voice, practice economy of speech, and trust emotions can bring the power of lay witness back into the worship service. Lay witnesses interjected into the preacher's sermons can help hearers to connect the dots between faith and practice. They also dramatize the shared leadership so crucial to the well-being of a small membership church. Lay witnesses before or after prayer, the offering, the Lord's Meal or baptism, or even in place of announcements would give visitors a glimpse into the soul of the congregation. A glimpse like that can incite a desire to belong. And belonging can lead to believing.

Postscript

Preaching in the Small Membership Church

Some who preach in small membership churches are laypersons with full-time jobs or careers elsewhere who exercise
their discipleship through a weekly cycle of preparing and
preaching sermons. Most who preach in small membership
churches are licensed local pastors who have been called away
from other jobs and careers at a mid or late season in their working life. Just enough time is left to grow into the weekly disciplines of the preaching life and become significantly better. The
rest of those who preach in small membership churches are
ordained persons whose commitment to preaching is larger than
the practice of preaching in any one location. Some of the hap-
piest of these are retired ordained persons who are discovering, or
rediscovering, after serving years in larger settings, the unique
pleasures of ministry in a small membership church.

Regardless of the level of their employment or preparation, all
of these preachers will be swept up in the challenges facing the
small membership church today: character issues like the congregation's poor self-image and dread of the future, skills issues like
the inadequate funding of ministry and dispirited worship, and
execution issues like sustaining multiple generations and the
contact with the crowds. Preaching in a small membership
church has a heroic quality about it today.

Most who preach in small membership churches for more than
a season know that work is needed in all three areas (character,
skills, and execution) but that the character issue must come first.
The preachers who are most invested in the fight to transform
small membership churches are those who view the condition of
their churches as an analogue to their own spiritual autobiogra-
phies. When they ask "how long can we hold out?" or "can these
dry bones live again?" they are asking about the force of character formed against discouraging odds.

It could be that big churches and megachurches are the wave of the Christian future. The dire predictions about small churches made by the prophets of church growth might be right, so we are indeed living in the last days of an endangered species. Perhaps all the king's horses and all the king's men cannot put together again the special combination of geographic, sociological, and historical forces that once favored the rise of small membership churches in this country. But we can't be sure. An historical view of, a global perspective on, and a theological respect for the small membership church argue against closing the doors too soon.

Meanwhile, the best of these preachers in small membership churches preach hope to their congregations and thereby to themselves. They have taken to heart the counsel of Paul, the missionary to a proliferating number of small churches, writing to Timothy, the set-apart preacher in one of those churches. "Proclaim the message; be persistent whether the time is favorable or unfavorable" (2 Timothy 4:2). They say about their congregations what they say about themselves as unfinished projects of God's grace. It isn't over until it's over.

Next-step Reading

1. The Preacher as Student of Scripture

Bandy, Thomas G. *Introducing the Uncommon Lectionary: Opening the Bible to Seekers and Disciples*. Nashville: Abingdon Press, 2006.

The New Interpreter's Bible: General Articles and Introduction, Commentary and Reflection for Each Book of the Bible, Including the Apocryphal/Deuterocanonical Books in Twelve Volumes. Nashville: Abingdon Press, 1994–2002.

Newsom, Carol A. and Sharon H. Ringe, eds. *The Woman's Bible Commentary*. Louisville: Westminster John Knox Press, 1992.

Patte, Daniel J., general editor, associate editors J. Severino Croatto, Nicole Wilkinson Duran, and Teresa Okure. *Global Bible Commentary*. Nashville: Abingdon Press, 2004.

Stookey, Laurence Hull. *Calendar: Christ's Time for the Church*. Nashville: Abingdon Press, 1996.

2. The Preacher as Anthropologist

Dudley, Carl S. *Effective Small Churches in the Twenty-first Century*, revised edition. Nashville: Abingdon Press, 2003.

Frank, Thomas Edward. *The Soul of the Congregation: An Invitation to Congregational Reflection*. Nashville: Abingdon Press, 2000.

Kemp, Bill. *Holy Places, Small Spaces: A Hopeful Future for the Small Membership Church*. Nashville: Discipleship Resources, 2005.

Pappas, Anthony G., ed., *Inside the Small Church*. Bethesda, Md.: Alban Institute, 2002.

Ray, David R. *The Indispensable Guide for Smaller Churches*. Cleveland: Pilgrim Press, 2003.

3. The Preacher as Writer

Bierly, Steve R. *How to Thrive as a Small-Church Pastor: A Guide to Spiritual and Emotional Well-Being*. Grand Rapids, Mich.: Zondervan, 1998.

Lamott, Anne. *Bird by Bird: Some Instructions on Writing and Life*. New York: Pantheon Books, 1994; Anchor Books Edition, 1995.

Lowry, Eugene L. *The Homiletical Plot*. Atlanta: John Knox Press, 1980.

Strunk, William, Jr., and E. B. White. *The Elements of Style*, 4th edition. Boston: Allyn and Bacon, 2000.

Taylor, Barbara Brown. *The Preaching Life*. Lanham, Md.: Rowman and Littlefield Publishers, 1993.

Wilson, Paul Scott. *The Four Pages of the Sermon: A Guide to Biblical Preaching*. Nashville: Abingdon Press, 1999.

4. The Preacher as Speaker

Bartow, Charles L. *God's Human Speech: A Practical Theology of Proclamation*. Grand Rapids, Mich.: William B. Eerdmans, 1997.

Childers, Jana. *Performing the Word: Preaching as Theatre*. Nashville: Abingdon Press, 1998.

Hogan, Lucy Lind and Robert Reid. *Connecting with the Congregation: Rhetoric and the Art of Preaching*. Nashville: Abingdon Press, 1999.

Sample, Tex. *Powerful Persuasion: Multimedia Witness in Christian Worship*. Nashville: Abingdon Press, 2005.

5. The Preacher as Storyteller

Anderson, Herbert and Edward Foley. *Mighty Stories, Dangerous Rituals: Weaving Together the Human and the Divine*. San Francisco: Jossey-Bass, 1998.

Burt, Steven E. and Hazel Ann Roper. *The Little Church That Could: Raising Small Church Esteem*. Valley Forge, Pa.: Judson Press, 2000.

Williams, Michael E., ed. *The Storyteller's Companion to the Bible*. vols. 1-7, 9-10, 12-13. Nashville: Abingdon Press, 1991–2005.

Wimberly, Edward P. *Recalling Our Own Stories: Spiritual Renewal for Religious Caregivers*. San Francisco: Jossey-Bass, 1997.

6. The Preacher as Theologian

Banks, Robert. *Paul's Idea of Community*. Peabody, Mass.: Hendrickson Publishers, 1994.

Migliore, Daniel L. *Faith Seeking Understanding: An Introduction to Christian Theology*. Second Edition. Grand Rapids, Mich.: William B. Eerdmans, 2004.

The Nature and Purpose of the Church. Faith and Order Paper 181. Geneva: World Council of Churches, 1998.

Robinson, Anthony B. *What's Theology Got to Do with It? Convictions, Vitality, and the Church*. Herndon, Va.: Alban Institute, 2006.

Willimon, William H. *Proclamation and Theology*. Nashville: Abingdon Press, 2005.

7. The Preacher as Leader

Hicks, H. Beecher. *Stormy Banks: Leading Your Congregation through the Wilderness of Change*. Grand Rapids, Mich.: Zondervan, 2004.

Schaller, Lyle E. *Small Congregation, Big Potential: Ministry in the Small Membership Church*. Nashville: Abingdon Press, 2003.

Weems, Lovett H., Jr. *Take the Next Step: Leading Lasting Change in the Church*. Nashville: Abingdon Press, 2003.

8. The Preacher as Pastor

Bonhoeffer, Dietrich. *Life Together*. Trans. John W. Doberstein. New York: Harper and Bros., 1954; HarperOne, 1978.

Lamott, Anne. *Traveling Mercies: Some Thoughts on Faith*. New York: Pantheon Books, 1999.

Nichols, J. Randall. *The Restoring Word: Preaching as Pastoral Communication.* San Francisco: Harper & Row, 1987.

Stookey, Laurence Hull. *Let the Whole Church Say Amen! A Guide for Those Who Pray in Public.* Nashville: Abingdon Press, 2001.

Wimberly, Edward. *Moving from Shame to Self-Worth: Preaching and Pastoral Care.* Nashville: Abingdon Press, 1999.

9. The Preacher as Prophet

Brueggemann, Walter. *The Prophetic Imagination,* 2nd ed.. Minneapolis: Fortress Press, 2001.

Hamilton, Adam. *Confronting the Controversies: Biblical Perspectives on Tough Issues,* rev. ed. Nashville: Abingdon Press, 2005.

McMickle, Marvin. *Where Have All The Prophets Gone? Reclaiming Prophetic Preaching in America.* Cleveland: Pilgrim Press, 2006.

Wesley, John. "The Late Work of God in North America," *The Works of John Wesley,* Volume 3, Sermons III (71–114), Sermon 114, 594–609.

Wuthnow, Robert and John H. Evans. *The Quiet Hand of God: Faith-Based Activism and the Public Role of Mainline Protestantism.* Berkeley: University of California Press, 2002.

10. The Preacher as Evangelist

Daniel, Lillian. *Tell It Like It Is: Reclaiming the Practice of Testimony.* Herndon, Va.: Alban Institute, 2005.

English, Donald. *An Evangelical Theology of Preaching.* Nashville: Abingdon Press, 1996.

Law, Eric H. C., *Inclusion: Making Room for Grace.* St. Louis: Chalice Press, 2000.

Swanson, Roger K. and Shirley F. Clement. *The Faith-Sharing Congregation: Developing a Strategy for the Congregation as Evangelist.* Nashville: Discipleship Resources, 1996.

Webber, Robert E. *Ancient-Future Evangelism: Making Your Church a Faith-Forming Community.* Grand Rapids, Mich.: Baker Books, 2003.

Notes

4. The Preacher as Speaker

1. John Wesley, "Directions Concerning Pronunciation and Gesture" in *The Works of the Reverend John Wesley, A. M.*, ed. John Emory (New York: Waugh and T. Mason, 1835), vol. 7, 487–93.

2. Ibid., 487.

3. Ibid., 487, 493.

4. Ibid., 492.

5. Ibid., 487.

6. Ibid., 491.

7. Ibid., 492.

8. Ibid., 493.

5. The Preacher as Storyteller

1. Phillips Brooks, *Lectures on Preaching* (New York: E. P. Dutton and Company, 1907), 5.

7. The Preacher as Leader

1. "History of East View EUB Church," by Ada M. (Hogue) Harbart, August 8, 1965, in *Stories from the Small Churches of the Wesleyan District, The West Virginia Conference of The United Methodist Church*, ed. Rebecca W. Scheirer, A Project of the Small Church Task Force of the Making Connections Initiative sponsored by a grant from the Lilly Foundation, Wesley Theological Seminary (May 2007): 17–18.

2. "Eldred United Methodist Church," compiled by Jean Hakes, edited by Kathie Martin and Dorie Heckman in Kane, May 17, 2007) in *Stories from the Small Churches of the Connellsville District, Indiana District, and Kane District of the Western Pennsylvania Conference of The United Methodist Church*, ed. Rebecca W. Scheirer, A Project of the Small Church Task Force of the Making Connections Initiative sponsored by

a grant from the Lilly Foundation, Wesley Theological Seminary (September 2007): 63.

3. "The Story of the Wiseburg Congregation" in *Stories from the Small Churches of the Baltimore North District, the Baltimore Washington Conference of The United Methodist Church*, ed. Rebecca W. Scheirer, A Project of the Small Church Task Force of the Making Connections Initiative sponsored by a grant from the Lilly Foundation, Wesley Theological Seminary (March 2007): 23–24.

9. The Preacher as Prophet

1. "Orlena United Methodist Church," in *Stories from the Small Churches of the Wesleyan District, The West Virginia Conference of The United Methodist Church*, ed. Rebecca W. Scheirer, A Project of the Small Church Task Force of the Making Connections Initiative sponsored by a grant from the Lilly Foundation, Wesley Theological Seminary (May 2007): 57.

2. Ibid.

10. The Preacher as Evangelist

1. "St. John's United Methodist Church" in *Stories from the Small Churches of the Harrisonburg District of The Virginia Conference of The United Methodist Church*, ed. Rebecca W. Scheirer, A Project of the Small Church Task Force of the Making Connections Initiative sponsored by a grant from the Lilly Foundation, Wesley Theological Seminary (November 2007): 12.

2. "Uriah United Methodist Church" in *Stories from the Small Churches of the Chambersburg District of The Central Pennsylvania Conference of The United Methodist Church*, ed. Rebecca W. Scheirer, A Project of the Small Church Task Force of the Making Connections Initiative sponsored by a grant from the Lilly Foundation, Wesley Theological Seminary (October 2007): 19.

3. "History of the Bendale United Methodist Church," Harriett Attanasio, in *Stories from the Small Churches of the Wesleyan District, The West Virginia Conference of The United Methodist Church*, ed. Rebecca W. Scheirer, A Project of the Small Church Task Force of the Making Connections Initiative sponsored by a grant from the Lilly Foundation, Wesley Theological Seminary (May 2007): 3.

4. In the literal Greek, "the, the crowd." The NRSV translates it as "the crowds," as in Matthew 14:13-21.